ISSUES IN
MARITIME CRIME

ISSUES IN MARITIME CRIME:

MAYHEM AT SEA

Edited by Martin Gill

Perpetuity Press

Perpetuity Press
PO Box 376
Leicester, LE2 3ZZ

First published 1995

All papers Copyright © Perpetuity Press 1995 except Cooper and Devlin which is © Crown Copyright 1995. Published with the permission of the Controller of Her Majesty's Stationery Office. The views expressed are those of the authors and do not necessarily reflect the views or policy of HM Customs and Excise or any other government department.

All rights reserved. Except for the quotation of short passages for the purposes of criticism and review, no part of this publication may be reproduced, stored in a retrieval system, or transmitted, in any form or by any means, electronic, mechanical, photocopying, recording or otherwise, without the prior written permission of the publisher or a licence from the Copyright Licensing Agency Limited. Details of such licences (for reprographic reproduction) may be obtained from the Copyright Licensing Agency Ltd, 90 Tottenham Court Road, London, W1P 9HE.

A catalogue reference for this book is available from the British Library

ISBN 1 899287 02 7 (paperback)

The views expressed in the papers are those of the authors and do not necessarily reflect those of Perpetuity Press

Typeset by J C Hart

Printed by R & G Design, Leicester

Perpetuity Press

Contents

Acknowledgements ii
List of contributors iii

INTRODUCING ISSUES IN MARITIME CRIME 1
Martin Gill

THE DIMENSIONS OF INTERNATIONAL MARITIME CRIME 4
Eric Ellen

INVESTIGATING MARITIME CRIME
—THE VIEW OF A LOSS ADJUSTER 12
Peter Clark

CONTAINERS AND CRIME
—AN IMPRACTICAL RESPONSE? 21
Ken Luck

HM CUSTOMS AND MARITIME CRIME 29
Paul Devlin and Robin Cooper

MARITIME CRIME AND PREVENTION
—A POLICE PERSPECTIVE 39
John Wilks

BOAT OWNERS AS CRIME VICTIMS
—PATTERNS OF VICTIMISATION 47
Martin Gill

MARITIME CRIME
—A BOAT OWNER'S PERSPECTIVE 58
Tim Goodhead

INDEX 65

Acknowledgements

The papers that appear in this volume were originally presented at a conference organised by the Centre for the Study of Public Order, University of Leicester. All the papers have been re-written and updated for this book, and thanks are due to all the contributors for their patience and assistance. I am also grateful for the advice of Jerry Hart, Nicholas Kasic, Peter Maxey and Jane Stevens. Robert Pugsley and former colleague Peter Francis played a large part in the early stages in helping me to progress with this venture. I am also indebted to Ben Fox for his advice and encouragement. Finally, a special thanks to Karen and Emily.

Martin Gill
Centre for the Study of Public Order
University of Leicester
January 1995

List of contributors

Peter Clark is a leading small craft Marine Loss Adjuster/Investigator in his own company, C Claims. He started working life in the insurance market before moving into the fibreglass industry. It was here he learned about boat construction and related engineering issues. After a spell back in the insurance industry working as an investigator on marine claims he decided to commit himself to this type of work. His investigations have taken him around the world.

Robin Cooper is Principal of the UK Branch of the Drugs Policy Division in Customs Headquarters. He previously held policy making posts in the VAT and Customs Directorates and worked as a uniformed preventive Customs Officer in Dover. Prior to joining HM Customs and Excise he spent nine years as a university lecturer in Morocco following the completion of a PhD in American Studies at Nottingham University in 1975.

Eric Ellen is Director of the ICC International Maritime Bureau which he set up in 1980. He was formerly Chief Constable of the Port of London Police and President of the International Association of Air and Sea Port Police. He is recognised as a world authority on aspects of maritime crime. He has been responsible for many developments in maritime security including the Counterfeiting Intelligence Bureau and the Commercial Crime Bureau. He has numerous publications to his credit.

Paul Devlin is a Senior Officer in Customs Headquarters, working in the Drugs Policy Division. His previous postings have involved working as a uniformed Customs Officer in Dover running a Drug Dog Unit and working as a VAT control officer and fraud investigator. He graduated in European Studies from Lancaster University in 1978.

Martin Gill is Deputy Director and Course Director of Security Management Studies at the Centre for the Study of Public Order at the University of Leicester. He completed his PhD in 1986 and became a Research Officer at the Centre for Criminology and Criminal Justice at the University of Hull, and later Lecturer in Criminology at the University of Wales, Cardiff. He has written widely on crime and security issues and recently edited a book, Crime at Work: Studies in Security and Crime Prevention, published by Perpetuity Press.

Tim Goodhead is Deputy Head of the Maritime Division of the Southampton Institute. He was formerly a Senior Lecturer in Property Management at the University of Portsmouth. Having a long-standing interest in maritime issues, he was an instructor and coach at the National Sailing Centre in Cowes, and Chief Instructor at Rockley Point Sailing School. He is presently leading a research project into aspects of maritime crime.

Ken Luck is an independent security consultant. He started life as a police officer and served for almost 30 years with the Port of London Police retiring as a Chief Superintendent. He then worked for an independent consultancy before spending five years as Assistant Director with the International Maritime Bureau in 1988. He has written numerous articles and is an internationally recognised expert on container security.

John Wilks is a serving police officer in Essex. He started life in the travel industry and in 1965 joined the British South Africa Police Force in Rhodesia. He returned to Britain three years later and joined the Essex police. In 1971 he was transferred to the Marine Unit where he has served ever since. This makes him one of the most experienced police officers in maritime crime in the country.

Introducing issues in maritime crime

Martin Gill

There is little agreement on what constitutes maritime crime. Broadly speaking it can include any criminal offence committed on or near the water, or against maritime equipment and maritime trade anywhere in the world. In practice it includes everything from petty vandalism on the river bank through theft of boats (which often takes on an international dimension), to fraud and piracy on the high seas. The papers in this volume reflect this diversity.

On the international stage there is no one agency responsible for collating details of maritime crime, and those that do so, including the International Maritime Organisation and the International Maritime Bureau, are hampered by the indifference, negligence and ignorance of many countries and agencies. Police forces in different countries all too frequently show a marked reluctance to co-operate in maritime matters[1]. Often victims are reluctant to report offences. Commercial victims fear that reporting crime will attract attention to an event which may undermine their clients' confidence in them. Often they fear that reporting offences would be too time consuming especially in the competitive world of international trade. Individuals who are victimised are sometimes apathetic when it comes to taking official action.

At the national level, and taking Britain as an example, official statistics nicely disguise the problem. Nevertheless, the step taken in 1994 to add a special category for boats to the Police National Computer (PNC) is a move in the right direction. A theft of a boat would have normally been classified under the general heading of 'theft of a conveyance' while theft from a boat would have appeared under 'other thefts'. With such statistics it is

---

[1] For a discussion see Gill, M. (1995) *Responding to Crime at Sea: A Forgotten Issue in Police Co-operation.* Crime, Order and Policing Occasional Paper. Centre for the Study of Public Order, University of Leicester.

1

impossible to define the extent of maritime crime or identify patterns of victimisation.

Yet there is evidence that at least some of the problems are getting worse. Certainly piracy re-emerged as a problem in the 1970s[2], and pirates continue to claim victims[3] while *The Times* reported that:

> Yacht thefts, smuggling and marine joy riding have increased so rapidly that the police national computer is being expanded to keep track of cases.
>
> *The Times*, 9 April, 1994

Such developments have hitherto not been matched by research. Nor are there evaluations of the appropriateness of various security measures, devices or procedures for different types of crime. The link between boat theft and other types of crime (including fraud, arson, piracy and drug trafficking) is rarely made. In this volume contributors have tackled these issues and referred to real life examples to illustrate their points.

The following papers were originally presented at a conference organised by the Centre for the Study of Public Order, University of Leicester. The object here is to raise awareness rather than present agreed viewpoints on current issues. Indeed, as will become clear, not all the authors agree on future developments (for example compare the views of Clark and Goodhead towards registration). Moreover, each presentation ends with a transcript of authors' responses to selected questions from the audience. It is hoped that this will provide an additional insight into some of the current thinking on a topic which has hitherto received scant attention.

In the first paper, Eric Ellen examines the international aspects of maritime crime and the links between trading fraud and piracy and murder. In looking at the ways of reducing the opportunities for such crime, Ellen directs attention to the role of governments, maritime organisations and banks. The international dimension is continued in the second paper where Peter Clark, a loss adjuster, discusses the theft of vessels, and the link with fraud and arson. He shows how the limitations of official documentation work to the advantage of international thieves.

---

[2] For a comprehensive examination of a range of maritime crimes see Mueller, G.O.W. and Adler, F. (1985) *Outlaws of the Ocean*. New York: Hearst Marine Books.

[3] Ellen, E. (1989) *Piracy at Sea*. Paris: International Chamber of Commerce, provides a broad discussion of the piracy problem and not least the extreme suffering of some piracy victims.

Introducing issues in maritime crime

An effective response to international maritime crime is dependent upon the introduction of appropriate security measures. In the third paper Ken Luck, an international authority on container crime, discusses the security value of containers. Luck traces the movement of products across the world and shows how the introduction of more sophisticated handling procedures reduces the security of cargo.

In the fourth paper Paul Devlin and Robin Cooper discuss the changing role of HM Customs in tackling maritime crime. In particular they discuss the ways in which their department is responding to the growing threat of drug trafficking, and highlight the value of intelligence which is dependent on effective collaboration with organisations and countries, especially in Europe. In the fifth paper John Wilks discusses the police response to maritime crime from his own experience as a police officer in Essex, England. His observations illustrate the shortcomings of the policies of many organisations (for example, insurance companies) designed to reduce crime. John Wilks is critical of a range of security measures presently being advocated.

The last two papers reflect the domestic threat posed by maritime offences. In the sixth, I discuss my findings from a survey of boat owners which show that levels of victimisation vary with the offence, the type of boat owned and also with the location. In addition, other findings suggest possible directions for crime prevention strategies. In the seventh and final paper Tim Goodhead examines crime from the perspective of the boat owner. It provides an insight into the benefits and limits of watch schemes, tagging devices and registration schemes. The paper challenges the view that boat owners are apathetic about security.

If maritime crime and responses to it are to be taken seriously they require a more candid discussion of the issues. If this volume facilitates even a small part of that process it will have achieved its principal objective.

The dimensions of international maritime crime

Eric Ellen

The topic of this paper is international fraud with special emphasis on international trading fraud and its connection with maritime crime. I shall discuss a number of aspects including piracy, diversion of vessels and so-called 'phantom' ships.

I will begin by relating the case of a ship owner in Australia who chartered his vessel to a person in Singapore. This person used the ship but failed to pay the owner, which, understandably, made him eager to get his ship back. He tried to trace his vessel for two years as it traded on the South China Seas. It was eventually arrested in Singapore but (as often happens) the ship broke arrest. The security guard on board went home and the ship simply disappeared again.

The ship was then purchased by a scrap merchant, who merely wanted to take the ship to China and scrap it. However, before he did so he wanted to remove all the items of value from the ship. When he came to the refrigeration room, he broke open the door and found ten dead bodies inside. When he reported the incident to the local police they apologised and said 'This is nothing to do with us; the incident occurred on the high seas'.

The ship had no registration, no flag and the scrap merchant had no idea what to do with the ten corpses. Who in the world was supposed to deal with problems of this nature? Eventually he sold the ship for scrap in China, although he is still trying to persuade the police to identify the dead bodies. How is it that in 1995 we have problems of this nature without a properly designated authority to provide a response?

I will return to this point later but for the moment let me turn to the problem of fraud and crime on a global basis. In 1985 it was estimated that maritime crime cost £13 billion per year.[4] This figure is growing at an alarming rate and London lawyers predict that their greatest increase will be in the

---

[4] Hansard, 12th February, 1985, pp. 311-320, *International fraud*.

negligence and property and fraud case loads. However, it is my belief that fraud cannot be responded to in isolation, as it is too often connected with other major crimes.

For example, last year a man contacted my organisation saying that he had been offered 50 containers of Marlboro cigarettes. Made in the United States by Philip Morris, Marlboro cigarettes are a very profitable commodity to buy. The 50 containers of cigarettes were to be loaded on the *Lisa Marie* in Miami, and our visitor wanted to know whether the deal was genuine.

We in the International Maritime Bureau were aware that this quantity of cigarettes would not normally be available for sale because such goods must be distributed while they are still fresh. As many as five surplus containers may become available from time to time; although 50 containers would not. He asked if the documentation he had been provided was genuine. It was relatively easy to identify as a fake as the 50 containers were consecutively numbered. This is a near-impossible occurrence, hence we were able to confirm that the deal was extremely suspect.

The Bureau has been able to frustrate a number of such frauds by assessing transactions for banks and other organisations and confirming that they are not genuine. However, we occasionally encounter major problems, a case in point involved a very important, influential and highly reputable United States carrier. It claimed to have loaded five containers of cigarettes on board a ship in Panama, and we were asked to ascertain whether this was true. We knew that it was not because the description of the cigarettes was entirely wrong, for reasons that must remain confidential. Yet here was a major carrier saying and reaffirming that it had loaded five containers on board a ship. Moreover, a major inspection company claimed that it had examined the cigarettes in Panama. But we knew that the cargo never existed.

One of the problems in the shipping industry is that goods and documents do not always match. This is a particular problem for banks as they have a duty to pay out cash on presentation of certain documents. In this particular instance the bank was under such an obligation unless some fault could be found with the documentation. We encouraged them to identify some minor error, and in the end the bank agreed to suspend payment until the ship had reached Antwerp.

In Antwerp, we were able to persuade customs officials to search the ship and they did indeed find five containers. However, all five were empty. This is a regular occurrence; frauds are a risk because of poor system checks that ensure the compatibility of goods and documents.

There are other examples. One country paid out for military goods that never existed. I possess the bill of lading, apparently issued by a famous and highly reputable Dutch company. The experienced eye can identify that the document is not genuine, but only in the light of the knowledge that this company does not carry arms and ammunition. The documentation was entirely fraudulent.

I have another document, a bill of laden ostensibly issued by the same Dutch company. We were called in to authenticate the papers, which concerned a shipping company in Shanghai. Again all seemed well, unless you are aware that there are no private shipping companies in Shanghai. That both sets of documents were fraudulent and both issued by the same people is vital information to the industry, and someone has to collate it. This is one of the Bureau's key functions.

Let me give you another example of our work. A man came into Heathrow Airport in 1991 travelling from Hong Kong to the United States. All he wanted was permission to stay in England for three days while he rested. However, when his passport was examined by immigration officers they noticed a stamp which showed he had entered the country through terminal two on a date when terminal two was closed.

The police were called and they searched his baggage and found US $250,000 in cash. This by itself is no crime, as you can bring as much money as you like into the United Kingdom. The only evidence they had of any offence committed was the passport containing the fraudulent stamp. In these circumstances all they could do was send him back to the country that had issued the passport. In this case it was Austria, so the police sent him to Vienna and advised their Austrian counterparts of his return. On arrival in Vienna he tried to book a flight to Nuremberg but was soon arrested. He turned out to be one of the most wanted men in Europe—Udo Proksch—a man who had tried to change his identity.

In 1977, Proksch sent a cargo of uranium from Italy to Hong Kong having insured it for 31 million Swiss Francs. Unfortunately, the cargo never reached its destination because the ship sank and six members of the crew of twelve drowned. Proksch claimed against his insurance for the 31 million Swiss Francs. However, police investigations discovered that what he had shipped was not a uranium processing plant, but old coal mining equipment which had no commercial value. It had been shipped to a Hong Kong company which had a two dollar capital.

So the police issued warrants for the arrest of Proksch and an accomplice on charges of purposely endangering lives by using explosives and attempted aggravated insurance fraud. But, remarkably, an army officer later claimed that he had supplied explosives to Proksch on the orders of a former government minister; indeed several members of the government were alleged to be implicated. All this happened in a European country.

Imagine this happening in the United Kingdom and the political storm it would cause. Proksch was unlucky—the ship was sunk in 1977 and in those days it was not possible to go to the bottom of the sea to investigate. By 1993 the necessary technology had been developed and experts discovered that the explosion had occurred within the ship. Proksch was eventually tried and convicted for murder and, following appeals, was sentenced to life imprisonment.

Another example is the so-called Cuban Coffee Caper In this case the Cubans wanted to buy coffee. You may ask why, when they produce a great deal of the commodity themselves. The answer is that they sell their quality products on the world market for as much as they can possibly get and buy cheaper beans for domestic use. When a West German commodity broker offered them coffee at US $110,000 below world prices, perhaps they should have looked twice, but they did not and agreed to proceed with the transaction.

The Cubans opened a letter of credit and agreed to pay nearly US $9 million through a bank in Canada. The arrangement was that when the seller could prove that the goods were aboard the ship, the bank would pay out the US $9 million.

In the event, the broker bought and insured an old ship, and whilst it was at the supposed port of loading he produced some documents to the bank and collected the US $9 million. The coffee, however, did not exist. Furthermore, besides embezzling the Cubans' money, the broker intended to sink the ship and collect the insurance.

In order to achieve his aim, the broker needed a scuttling crew, that is a crew to carry out the crime. Scuttling crews can be hired in ports throughout the world; you quite literally hire four to six people to take the ship out to sea and deliberately sink it. Fortunately, this is a rare occurrence.

However, before the ship was taken out, the Cubans found out that it was empty and the broker was later arrested in Miami. He had a condominium, a yacht, a car, pockets full of money and a lifestyle that can only be described as luxurious. You would have expected him to have got his full desserts for such a crime; perhaps nine or ten years in prison. He was convicted, sentenced to only two years' imprisonment, then deported after serving only two months. US $9 million for two months in prison!

Contrast that with recent events in a predominantly Islamic country, where two people convicted of maritime crime were each ordered to have an arm and leg removed (although not from the same side). I am not advocating this as just, but we must encourage the judiciary to impose effective punishments in such cases. I also believe that the industry itself must act against the problem, because when it stands up and does something the problem goes away.

Let me give you an example. Fifty ships disappeared in the Far East within the same two-year period. This worried insurers, so they put their hands in their pockets and produced US $50,000 to form the Far Eastern Regional Investigating Team (FERIT) to investigate the problem. They made some interesting discoveries. Of the 50 disappeared ships, 28 had gone missing in mysterious circumstances. Furthermore, scuttling or deliberate sinking could be proved in thirteen instances and FERIT discovered that most of the vessels were, in fact, small and ageing.

They also found that most of the ships flew the Panamanian flag and had what we call the Japanese class of inspection, which is not surprising considering the location of the ships and the area of enquiry. The insurers' response was to issue instructions for goods not to be carried by small ships flying the Panamanian flag. As a result such scuttlings did not reoccur for the next ten years. The insurers had considered the problem from a rational perspective, then invested in an effective response.

Current problems often involve what we refer to as 'phantom' ships. This type of event is best described by illustration. It is possible to go to a hotel overlooking Manila Bay and simply order a ship to be stolen. It costs around US $350,000 for a gang of pirates to steal the ship. If you want the crew left on board, they will leave them there. If you don't want the crew on board, the pirates will simply throw them into the sea. Nine seamen lost their lives in this way in the Southern Philippines not so long ago.

The 'buyers' simply obtain a false registration for the vessel which then visits ports throughout the world, collecting cargoes before disappearing with them. Recently one of these phantom ships picked up a cargo from Vietnam. Instead of taking the cargo to India, for where it was intended, they took it to Manila. We became aware of the incident and went to Manila to recover the cargo. It had been discharged at a free port to a warehouse owned by a Japanese company. We went to the courts and asked them to release the cargo to us, but eight months later we had to do a deal with the fraudsters to buy the cargo back. It sounds incredible but there was simply no other way to recover the goods—we were hampered by officials so our clients instructed us to make a deal.

International fraud is very difficult to combat, but international piracy is perhaps even worse. In the Malacca Strait, quite near to Singapore, there were 200 piratical attacks in 1991. The *modus operandi* was to tie up the master and senior members of the crew before stealing goods from the ship's safe and the crew. Losses were less than US $20,000 a time, but such attacks leave ships without navigation in very narrow navigable waters with every chance of a major disaster.

The Indonesians have made a number of arrests which has reduced the problem. However, not so long ago the master of a ship in the Straits was given a note which read 'I need all your money, if you do not like hurt no speak, follow order, also you take crew money'. The master, who was British, went to the safe and he opened it for the pirates. There was too little room in the cabin for both of them so he stepped back and allowed the pirate to enter the safe. The master took advantage of an opportunity to escape and ran away, but he was chased by the pirates who shot him dead. The chief officer met the same fate. The Indonesian authorities took the ship and, following a thorough enquiry, concluded that this was a case of mutiny rather than piracy. This verdict caused uproar in the shipping industry.

The pattern of piracy is changing. We are now getting attacks in the triangle formed by Hong Kong, Hainan and Luzon. About 35 ships in the latter part of 1992 and 1993 were chased by other ships firing machine guns, rockets, and other weapons. The attackers were definitely identified as Chinese—a fact which caused a major political problem in the region.

The International Maritime Organisation has set up a Working Group to look at the problem. They have produced a report which offers some advice to ship owners and crews, but I ask myself whether what is needed is more effective law enforcement. There are few agencies as competent as the Dutch police. We do have a few units in the United Kingdom, but internationally it is very difficult to get people, police officers in particular, even to understand the problem let alone to deal with it. Many of the frauds cross numerous international boundaries causing major problems for law enforcement.

In 1978, I was Chief Constable of the Port of London Police and the President of an organisation called the International Association of Air Port and Sea Port Police. In 1979 I raised these policing and enforcement issues and I began to get letters from all over the world from people who had similar problems.

I even went to Interpol and asked them to set up a dedicated International Maritime Bureau, but for political reasons they could not do so. Then I received a call from the International Chamber of Commerce in Paris (one of the world's most prestigious business organisations), who asked what I would do about the problem of fraud. I suggested the Bureau idea to them so they invited me to set one up. I accepted their invitation and retired from the police service in 1981.

We now deal with approximately 130 cases per year of the type I have described. We have also been instrumental in setting up an anti-piracy centre in Malaysia which is working very well. I believe that each piratical act should be independently investigated. If they are not some countries will do their own thing and will produce the wrong results for the wrong reasons. This is a major problem. The industry is very slow to respond and you have to hit those concerned hard to make them realise that they have a problem and harder still to get them to do something about it.

Discussion

Q. You mentioned the point that the punishment should fit the crime and you gave two extreme examples. You are not advocating that we take arms and legs off, are you?

A. I am not advocating that the law be changed in any way. The law is adequate. It is merely that in the case I mentioned the judges could have given a sentence that was more fitting to the crime. No-one would have complained about five years (including the prisoner), but it's a nonsense to give two years imprisonment with just two months inside.

Q. Who funds you? And do you deal only with commercial craft? I would be more interested in ocean-going yachts and other craft that we deal with in our harbours. Does that come into your realm at all?

A. On the 5th January 1994 the Bureau introduced the International Yacht Registry to respond to the growing number of thefts. We believe this is a major problem but it is nothing compared with the problem of maritime fraud, where every case we deal with involves up to US $5 million, so that has had a priority until now. But with piracy, we began to look at yachts and then decided on the Yacht Register. We are funded by members, including banks and insurance companies, traders and governments. We have a resolution at the United Nations, which calls upon governments and law enforcement agencies to work with us. We are a non-profit making organisation.

Q. Thinking of American owners that I know, when they move their boats down to Japan, they take on board mercenaries who act as watch dogs or security guards. Many of them are ex-British army carrying automatic rifles. The owners have to resort to that.

A. I regularly receive calls from former SAS people and others that want to do this work. Normally, the major shipping companies will not pay for it. The small yacht owners may well do so. But I would be very wary about using firearms in somebody else's territorial waters. You would soon be locked up and charged with major crimes, and face terrible problems.

Investigating maritime crime—the view of a loss adjuster

Peter Clark

A loss adjuster is a person appointed by an insurance underwriter to investigate insurance claims made by policyholders. More specifically the loss adjuster must report on the admissibility of any loss and make recommendations on settlement. All this is undertaken in an impartial and unbiased manner. Indeed, although the fee is paid by the underwriters, the aim is to ensure fair play to the policyholders and shareholders of the insurance company or the underwriting syndicate. A loss adjuster has a duty to ensure fair and reasonable settlements and thus maintain a control on premium levels.

Our working life is one of constant surprise and change. Every day underwriters receive many different claims; from a minor collision to the theft of a whole craft. We are instructed to deal with these as they come into the claims departments and to contact the claimants directly, then to resolve their problems individually. Frequently investigations involve travel overseas, often in Europe and sometimes as far away as the Caribbean. In this paper I will discuss marine investigations, identifying some of the issues and problems. I propose to concentrate on the main categories of loss starting with theft and working through to fraud and arson.

Thefts

Small craft theft is not a new problem. It has occurred all over the world for as long as there have been boats. However, since World War II the West has enjoyed a new level of prosperity and popular leisure pursuits such as boating have grown proportionately. It is within the scope of many families to own a small pleasure yacht. Marinas have been built to accommodate this growth. Accessories such as electronic navigation aids, radar, radio, etc. have become available at a relatively modest cost and so the marine world has developed its own consumer society.

The criminal fraternity have not failed to see the attraction either. Most yachts, motor cruisers, speed boats, etc. include relatively valuable and portable items, yet rarely do they have adequate security measures. Usually they are moored by no more than a few ropes and visited at most once or twice a week; they lie unattended, insecure and begging the attention of the unscrupulous. The theft of yachts and small craft is a world-wide problem. I have concrete data on this since I recently attended a conference of the National Association of Marine Investigators in New Orleans.

In the year ending November 1992, 30,800 boats were stolen in the USA out of a total boating population estimated at between thirteen and nineteen million—depending on how one defines a boat, e.g. whether one includes boats under fifteen feet. The worst affected state is Florida which suffered losses of 5,313 boats. Texas and California were a close second and third with 3,300 and 3,000 losses of small craft.

In the USA I believe the police estimate that their recovery rate for stolen boats is approximately 30 per cent over all. In the UK I estimate a recovery rate for smaller craft, that is of less than 20 feet, of approximately 20-25 per cent, while for larger craft it is about 60 per cent. It is harder in the UK to estimate the figures as there is no centrally co-ordinated system of reporting all marine thefts. The Metropolitan Police have set up a Marine Computer Database in the Thames Division which it is hoped will provide such data in the not too distant future. From the insurance perspective, my company 'C Claims' deals with approximately 1,000 theft losses a year, ranging from the smallest jet ski to the largest luxury sailing yacht and motor cruiser. Individual losses range from around £2,000 to £1 million although the average value of losses these days are estimated at between £5,500 and £7,000.

In Europe the problem is very similar and our Scandinavian, Dutch, French, German and Italian counterparts report comparable patterns of loss. Where does the stolen craft go? Most of the smaller craft re-circulates to the consumer within a year and often remains within a 50-mile radius of their original location. They surface in various ways; through boat auctions, classified advertisements, marine dealers and so on. The public buy these craft usually quite innocently and because of the lack of formal registration requirements in the UK they have no clue as to the vendors' integrity. Whilst registration will not in itself prevent crime it will certainly help.

We have seen an increasing trend for stolen craft to be smuggled abroad. They are sold—again often to an innocent consumer—or used to assist in the commission of other crimes, such as drug smuggling. Larger craft usually head south to the Mediterranean where once again they end up with an innocent purchaser. Various registration systems apply throughout Europe. In the UK formal registration is more common for larger craft via the British Shipping Registry but sadly this does not provide any deterrent in itself. We also have a Small Ships Register now operated by the Drivers Vehicle Licensing Centre at Swansea. The resulting document allows the boat owner to go abroad without the need for payment of import duties, etc. These documents are widely abused by thieves. Frequently, and incredibly, the yacht thief applies for the Small Ships Registration document before the boat is stolen—it is that easy to obtain. The British Ships Register is for larger vessels and it provides a document of title. The documentation from both registers looks official but it implies more authority than actually exists and is exploited by thieves.

Fraud: scuttling and arson

Fraud is not a new phenomenon but it has increased. As more people have got away with it so others have been encouraged to follow suit. Statistics are hard to substantiate, but we detect fraud and prosecute alleged thefts many times a year. We assume that these are the tip of the iceberg. Insurers must protect their policyholders and shareholders by investing more resources in the investigation and prevention of theft and fraud.

Alleged sinkings which result in total losses are a serious problem for the insurance industry. This is especially the case in a time of serious economic recession when levels of honesty are sometimes lowered. I do not propose to deal with the genuine accidental losses that occur, only with the deliberate scuttling of vessels for insurance claims. Every year we are seeing an increasing number of scuttlings, but the number and cumulative value are difficult to gauge since there is no central collation of statistics.

The Marine Accidents Investigation Board does have reliable figures for the total number of reported incidents. As specialists we have attempted to develop, amongst other things, a unique computer database of stolen craft and equipment. The database extends back to the late 1970s although it is more comprehensive from the 1980s onwards. We are now in the process of combining this information with that of our European counterparts to form a central European database of stolen boats and their equipment. There is much progress to be made here.

Similarly, there is an urgent need to review how law enforcement agencies in the UK approach these matters. All too often there is no system in place for either the coastguard, marine surveyors or police to co-ordinate enquiries of this nature. We are convinced from our experience that many so-called accidental sinkings of expensive pleasure craft and small commercial craft are deliberate and carried out purely for the purpose of claiming insurance.

Let me quote you an example which I dealt with. I have altered the locations because of continuing litigation. In early 1987 I received an instruction from an insurer to investigate the sinking of a 50-foot fishing vessel. The insured person did not personally use the craft but appointed a skipper and crew to use it for fishing. The vessel operated unsuccessfully in the south and so it was decided to take it north to try and make this £90,000 investment pay. Months went by and little income was produced. A plan was hatched by the skipper and the owner to scuttle the boat. When interviewed, first by the police and then by me, the crew gave a full account of what they said had been a very successful fishing trip. They said they were trying to work the craft at all hours in an effort to earn a living. They gave me a full and compelling account of their experiences in the life raft. However, certain aspects of the story suggested to me that this matter required fairly careful scrutiny and I pursued a number of avenues of enquiry.

I found to my concern that the owner of the vessel was heavily involved with a bankrupt car dealer who had an extremely poor financial track record. Then approximately four weeks after initiating the enquiry I received a telephone call at my office on a Friday afternoon. It was from a person calling himself John who wanted to talk to me about this investigation. He told me that in fact the craft had been completely stripped of all its equipment including the engine long before the sinking. The craft had been towed out under cover of darkness. He took me to a fishing vessel in the harbour owned by one of the crew who was on board the boat when it supposedly went down. On board we found many of the electrical items from the vessel, as well as a chart showing the precise positions which they had mapped for the sinking. This evidence was recovered and the police were immediately alerted. Enquiries have led to the various conspirators being tried, and although there were some frustrations in the process I am pleased to say that we secured a conviction. At present this is being challenged by one of the group, hence the continuing litigation.

Sometimes fraud is related to arson. The initial work in a fire investigation is the most important. Good note-taking, photographic work and attention to detail are fundamental. If, as an adjuster, I have a suspicion of arson, I have to consider immediately the appointment of a forensic expert to determine the cause and to provide us with a report. Close liaison with the police and fire brigade is also essential. In my experience most European countries, particularly those of Northern Europe, have a very good understanding of the arson problem and are most willing to participate in a full and thorough enquiry.

I was recently involved in a suspected arson case in Scandinavia in which two vessels were totally destroyed. Damage totalling £150,000 was caused and there was little doubt in the minds of all investigating bodies that arson had occurred. It has, however, proved far more difficult to determine the complicity of the insured person or his associates. In most cases, unless there is proof of a breach of policy warranty or non-disclosure, underwriters may be obliged to meet what they strongly believe to be a contrived loss. The main difficulty in the Scandinavian case has been to disprove 'alibi evidence' provided by the insured person concerning his or her whereabouts immediately prior to the fire. We are convinced nonetheless that the owner was present at the scene about an hour or so before the fire started.

I recall another example which involved a fire on a laid-up motor cruiser. It was on blocks in the insured person's garden. I was quickly convinced that arson had occurred. I was very suspicious of the policyholder and immediately requested the assistance of a forensic expert who confirmed my impression. I also approached an expert in wooden boat construction who determined that the vessel contained terminal rot from stem to stern. Later, as I scrutinised the bill of sale I found that the price shown had been altered from £2,000 to £12,000; the forgery was extremely convincing. We went to trial and secured a guilty plea and a £2,000 fine alongside a suspended custodial sentence. Had we not found the documentary fraud, however, the case could not have been launched.

Towards crime prevention

Since 1972 all production craft in the USA have had to be marked with a hull identification number. This number is intended to be indelibly marked on the hull with a duplicate number being inscribed in a hidden position elsewhere on the hull. All outboard motors and inboard engines also carry serial numbers as do the trailers on which the boats are carried. In some states, known as 'title' states, it is compulsory to register a vessel through a coastguard agency. The USA has thus organised the management and protection of small recreational craft on a very disciplined basis. The authorities have endeavoured to register these vessels in such a way as to protect the public from thieves and unscrupulous dealers. A further advantage is that they are more easily able to operate product safety recalls.

Nevertheless, boat theft is a thriving industry and the system itself cannot prevent theft. In Europe, as I have said, there is a lack of co-ordination. Even if the small craft world were regulated with a system of registration, I doubt whether the motive would be mainly the prevention of marine theft. Registration would facilitate some form of taxation by the authorities.

Nevertheless, it is necessary in what is a costly and dangerous pursuit. The role of the European Union is important here.

The identification of small craft needs to be made easier. Even a small commercial vessel such as a trawler can be anonymous from the dock side, and searching a marina for a production yacht is, even to the initiated, like looking for a needle in a haystack. We have observed a number of attempts to improve the way in which vessels are identified, and we know that the police force in Hampshire have a project in hand which we hope will provide some ideas.

In the USA a number of attempts have been made to draw up guidelines. Indeed the National Association of Marine Investigators has produced a comprehensive booklet on methods of identifying boats. This assists us greatly, particularly with US manufactured vessels. Remember, however, that there are 13,000 manufacturers of small craft in the USA; many of these are backyard operations turning out no more than three or four boats a year. It is therefore difficult to produce a guide to the identification of more than regular production craft, and even then there is no certainty of continuity of identification numbers or serial numbers.

Even when vessels are located by an agency, be it the police or another group, there is a need for quick, efficient, and accurate communication between the police forces and other agencies involved, no matter how far apart they may be and no matter how diverse their systems. We all know of Interpol which is intended to be the medium through which enquires between international police forces should be directed. In practice, while there is a specialist section dealing with marine losses, achieving a swift response is almost impossible. Often the delays are not in Interpol but in our own bureaucratic systems.

At the international level, each country needs to review the way in which it handles specialised police enquiries. Thieves know no boundaries and no jurisdiction. It must be a world-wide objective to make the process of law enforcement more direct and more efficient. This is a need of which my company is acutely aware. We often become involved in recoveries that present an amalgam of jurisdiction problems, and through our ability to go directly to the respective agencies we strive to cut out the delays that can prejudice the recovery of marine property and the apprehension of the criminal.

For example, we recently recovered a number of jet skis, trailerable speed boats, motor cruisers and motor vehicles stolen from the UK, France, Italy and elsewhere. These items were found, through an informant's tip-off, on a Mediterranean island. The thieves were mainly British subjects. The various police authorities had a problem since no one agency had an obvious reason to take the lead in the enquiry. Furthermore, budgetary constraints applied; to send one or two officers to a Mediterranean island and then perhaps to France, Italy, etc. places a substantial burden on the system, yet ultimately that is what is required. We were able to react immediately and to co-ordinate the response of each police agency. Thus there can be a place for the private sector to act as a catalyst and speed the process of justice. Co-operation of this kind marks a way forward in investigations. Incidentally, this operation was one of many in which we are involved and it led to the recovery of £500,000 worth of property.

Discussion

Q. You spoke about compulsory registration and boat marking which have taken place in America. The results have been very positive yet it has not been introduced into Britain. This was my most surprising finding when I first started looking at registration. It seems to me that the answer is simple: just copy the Americans. Why is there so much resistance to this?

A. There are a lot of reasons for this resistance but before I answer the question I think I should just remind you that Britain is an odd country in Europe. We drive on the wrong side of the road. We are also an island race. We tend to think differently. In any event we have a very sophisticated computer running the car registration system yet all this does not prevent car theft. By the same token registration will not prevent boat theft. What it will do, if we can regularise the system somewhat, is give the average member of the public a better chance. But you will not prevent boat theft by registration *per se*.

Q. Why do we not have registration?

A. There is a resistance on the part of the public and particularly the Royal Yachting Association. The RYA resist compulsory registration for reasons related to civil liberties. They regard it as an infringement of civil liberty and I can understand and sympathise with the argument. However, what they do not see are the victims, the people that I have to go and deal with.

Q. But why is it any more an infringement on your civil liberty than having your car registered for example?

A. Precisely. I could not agree more. This is an issue Tim Goodhead will take up later: it is linked to a perception that there should be complete freedom at sea.

Q. The American statistics prove that their system is no better than ours. Over 30,000 boats stolen and only 30 per cent recovered is, as you have said, in line with the situation in this country. Registration and marking does not appear to help from what you have said. Is that correct?

A. I am not proud of the results. We have a bigger problem because we have a much more diverse coastline, and we have jurisdiction problems. We do very well and we are lucky that it is not worse. I think registration in the States curtailed an otherwise spiralling problem. We have got to start to address the problem now otherwise our position will spiral too.

Q. You have to sort the wheat from the chaff. In America you will probably find that of the 30,800 thefts, probably 85 per cent will be of jet skis and speed boats.

A. I can tell you it is actually 14 per cent.

Q. The other thing which I think is important but which you did not bring up in your statistics is that where I operate, in the South West, the biggest area of crime is theft of equipment, that is outboard motors from boats, and people going into boats and stealing radar, navigation equipment, etc. rather than actually stealing the boat.

A. The average yacht owner has very little concern about security. Furthermore, neither have manufacturers.

Q. I have to say that we manufacture marine security systems and the total apathy that we find from the UK insurance bodies amazes me. Insurance companies are not particularly bothered whether an owner fits security measures to his boat, whereas in Europe it tends to be different.

A. The problem with the insurance industry in this country, and I think it is true of most countries, is that they are competitive. Thus if one insurance company offers terms which effectively cuts their premium income without an obvious gain then really he cuts his own throat. I personally think that all proposal forms for insurance of a small craft should require a full complement of serial numbers because by that means you have at least one fixed record.

Q. If you want to insure a Mercedes or a Ford Cosworth the insurance company will require a particular type of alarm system fitted. Most of these cars are in the £20,000 to £30,000 bracket, and yet the same insurance companies insuring a £750,000 boat will not require any system fitted. At the moment we are involved with a group who have a top of the range boat with a lock on the door that costs £7.50.

A. The insurance companies think that they are in a competitive market in the marine world but take a different view when insuring cars.

Q. One thing I would like you to explain is the system you mentioned being operated by Hampshire Constabulary.

A. It is not publicised yet because it is still in its infancy. They have got the main idea and it is a very good one. It is a 30 or 40 page booklet following very much the American example. It is a manual to help police officers to identify boats. This is a problem because an identification number can be hidden in any number of six or seven places; there isn't a particular pattern. Also in this country we have not adopted the ICOMIA[5] standard. For three or four years now we have been supposed to be following the same example, all our boats are supposed to be issued with a number on the transom and a hidden number. In practice I find many boats are not being issued with those numbers.

Q. It is a two-prong attack; it is really education, isn't it? It is educating the boat owner as to how to keep their boat, and educating the insurance companies to act as a body and to ensure that boats are registered and protected in some way.

A. Exactly. I think that it's a good move that the DVLC have taken over the operation of the Small Ships Register. It does now mean that there is a means by which you can start to regulate. If Brussels directs we can then enforce registration upon all boats, say all those over 15 feet. I come back to what I said before—it will not stop theft but it will mean that you have another way of handling the problem.

Q. How often does a claimant get the full value of their boat back, even if it is insured?

A. Well, that is another debate. Very often the insured value exceeds the true market value of the craft. If this is the case it provides a great incentive for people to make fraudulent claims. This is an area where I feel the insurance industry must make rapid changes.

---

[5] For further details of the ICOMIA standard contact the British Marine Industries Federation, Meadlake Place, Thorplea Road, Egham, Surrey. TW20 8HE.

Containers and crime— an impractical response?

Ken Luck

This paper is divided into three parts. First, I shall look at the reasons for the existence of container crime; second, I shall consider some case studies which help to illustrate the problems of prevention and detection; third, I shall focus on some of the realities of preventing container crime.

When containers first arrived, in the 1960s, they were considered to be the answer to all the ills of cargo transportation. You could move cargo, in quantity, speedily, economically and without danger of damage or crime. Admittedly pilferage has fallen away but the determined criminal is never going to be beaten completely; invariably offenders will change their technique. They did this quite quickly. They corrupted the system and turned it to their own advantage.

Determining the extent of container crime is problematic. We do not know how much crime there is because there are no centrally recorded statistics. However, a recent exercise with a North American insurer concluded that container crime incurred a world-wide cost of US $285 million each year. I will not name the insurer or go into details here regarding how this sum was computed; suffice to say that it is probably an underestimate. However, it is still a considerable sum and, most interestingly, the greater part of this crime is preventable.

So why does container crime occur? The answer lies in the inability of business to translate the conventional cargo handling system into the container age. It is worth pausing to consider this system in more detail. Let us imagine there is a consignor who wishes to move 1,000 cartons. One day a lorry will arrive at his premises and load the goods. They will be counted by a clerk on behalf of the company and also by the driver of the lorry. Each will check the other's work and both will consider the quantity and the condition of the goods.

All being well the lorry driver will then deliver the load to the dock shed and again both the driver and the loading clerk will count the contents, each cross-checking the other. The cartons, while being stored, will be subject to check counts, particularly when the goods are valuable. Once the ship arrives the goods will be trucked to the quayside and again they will be counted by a representative of the port authority and by a clerk on behalf of the sea carrier. The cargo then makes its sea voyage and, at the country of delivery, the whole process undertaken in the country of origin is repeated again. This means that from the consignor to consignee the load may well have been counted up to 20 times, and each count will have included a check for condition and quantity.

Let us imagine a theft while the cargo is stowed in the port area. Let us say that the shed staff see 1,000 cartons in stowage when they go home one evening, but on arrival the next day they find a hole in the shed roof and only 900 cartons. Now there is a clue there somewhere! These facts establish the when, where and how, and it is up to the investigators to discover the who. We know the loss occurred between the last correct and first incorrect count—overnight. It establishes liability and responsibility. In addition, it identifies the law enforcement agency responsible for investigating the theft. This point is crucial and I shall return to this later.

Let us move forward and repeat the shipment but with the goods in a container. In these circumstances, with a full container load, the consignor will, in all probability, assume responsibility for loading the container and for all checks. The driver may not even be present at the time. The consignor will fit the seal and eventually the driver will collect one container 'said to contain ...'. The container will then be transported to the terminal and eventually on to a ship bound for the receiving country. There this procedure is reversed until, in the fullness of time, the container is opened at the premises of the consignee and the goods are unpacked.

One can see, therefore, that the goods are counted into the container and eventually counted out again, but they are not subject to checks in between. This is the very essence of the container system.

Let us imagine a theft again and at the same place as last time. If the criminals manage to gain access to the container and get out again without being seen the incident will not be acknowledged until the container reaches the consignee. This may be days and thousands of miles later. When the loss is discovered, using the principle 'between the last correct and first incorrect count' we have a theft anywhere between consignor and consignee. Responsibility and liability are difficult to determine and, which is of prime importance, it is impossible to identify any single law enforcement agency having responsibility to investigate the crime. The result is quite simply that no-one deals with it.

Some will no doubt want to ask about the seal. The security seal system has fallen into virtual disuse or irrelevance. When I left the police service some thirteen years ago there was not a container seal on the market that I could not open and close again, and no-one would have been aware that I had tampered with it. To be fair things have improved a little, but seals are far from perfect. In addition to these shortcomings, a seal is only of use if it forms part of a disciplined system. The very essence of this system is that there should be an examination of the seal at every point of interchange with the examination covering both the identity and the integrity of the seal. This just is not practical.

A major concern is safety. For a seal to be properly examined requires a human being to alongside the container at the moment of receipt. This used to be the practice in the Port of London but quaysides are dangerous places. During my association with the port three tally clerks were killed while examining seals. Many argued, quite understandably, that safety considerations deserved priority over those of security.

In a different way operational considerations have overtaken security. In the early days, containers moved and were handled in almost the same way as conventional cargo, albeit that the bulk was greater. Nowadays some highly mechanised ports receive ships with containers stacked five high on deck. They are removed by a special crane and stowed five high on the shore, and will eventually be trans-shipped again five high on deck. This could mean that when entering and exiting the port a container will never be closer than 40 feet to the ground. How then does a clerk examine the seals?

There is also the question of liability. If a port authority can in some way avoid all liability for the containers' contents, then why should it adopt procedures which may impose a liability; one which contractually it is not required to assume? The Port of Singapore is a prime example in that its liability is nil, as stipulated by the enabling legislation. There are also some carriers who adopt the principle of 'we receive a box—we handle a box—we deliver a box—we are not responsible for quantity or condition of content'. With this philosophy it is not difficult to see why a seal checking system is considered an irrelevance. What this means is that the determined thief can steal from a container virtually anywhere and the fact will not be noticed until final discharge.

In any event the quality of seals is almost an irrelevance in terms of container security. The determined criminal will access the container without even touching the seal. The main problem for the industry is that the sealing system is an add-on to the bolting mechanism. The bolting mechanism has points of articulation and by attacking these, for example by removing and replacing bolts, it is possible to break into and re-close the container. There will be no trace on the seal and this is true whether it is of the penny indicative type or the high security type; it will not be touched.

Over the last year or so there has been a further development: when there is an unexplained deficiency in the contents of a container we tend to think of fraud as much as theft. In circumstances where the consignor and consignee are part of the same ethnic group or they are otherwise connected we think of fraud before we think of theft. The criminal has been quick to realise that if the system disguises the fact that goods have been removed, it can equally disguise the fact that they were never there in the first place. In many cases of fraud we have a conspiracy between the two ends of the system to defraud the insurer or carrier in the middle.

Here are some examples. A couple of years ago a container was loaded inland in Brazil; 265 cartons of cameras with two shippers' seals applied. The container went by road to Santos, then by German vessel to Hamburg, by rail to Stuttgart and then by road to the consignee, which was the same company as the consignor. At its final destination the seals were intact.

On opening the container it was found that there were no cartons of cameras, instead there were eleven large pieces of steel piping. Now according to the documents this could not happen. The container was sealed at the time of loading and the seals were still intact on delivery, yet a crime had been committed. It was my responsibility to carry out an investigation to establish whether the sea carrier was in any way liable for the loss.

In this case we were fortunate. Those criminals who think they are clever and replace stolen property with other material to make-up the weight are in fact stupid. Frequently, the examination of replaced material that gives a very precise indication of the place of theft. In this case the steel piping was scrap but contained traceable bore marks; but the main clue came from the lengths of timber which had been used to prevent the pipes from rolling about. It was found that these timbers had been nailed to the floor of the container using a nail manufactured in North America. However, the timber was Brazilian oak which, circumstantially at least, put the point of crime before the shipment from Brazil. Although the ship's documents claimed that the containers had been sealed immediately after loading, quite evidently something else must have happened, and the documentation was wrong.

In the above example the goods did exist but they were stolen. In the next example the goods never existed in the first place. Here, five containers of jeans were shipped in the same vessel from Venezuela to three different consignees in Italy. When they landed at Genoa, the containers were found to be empty. Although the containers had been manifested as sealed, four were unsealed. Theft was suspected.

An early breakthrough in the investigation came when it was noticed that the 40-foot container was recorded as containing 48,000 pairs. One telephone call established that the maximum quantity of jeans which can be loaded into a 40-foot container is 22,000 pairs. Thus the greed of the fraudster was the beginning of his undoing. Enquiries focused on the Venezuelan 'exporter' and in the fullness of time his whole 'organisation' was revealed to be a flimsy front set up for the purposes of this fraud; and indeed all the documentation had been forged.

This still leaves the question of the four unsealed and one sealed container. It must be understood that when one is in the world of multi-million dollar crime it is possible to buy almost anyone to do anything. It is possible to arrange to have someone remove seals aboard ship. This is what is presumed to have happened in this case. This would put the liability firmly at the door of the carrier. However, we believe, although we can't prove it, that only four of the containers could be found or reached, and the fifth had to be left with the seal on.

The following case, which occurred about three years ago, is an example of opportunistic fraud. A container was loaded in Spain with leather garments that were produced in that country. The total value was well in excess of US $1 million. The container was sealed with a shipper's seal at the point of loading and then taken to Valencia for shipment. By the time it arrived in Beirut it had what is called an alien seal, that is a different seal to the one that was applied by the shipper. The importer called for a survey which showed that the contents had been pilfered and there was a 96 per cent shortage. Pilfered means that while the packaging was present, the contents of the individual cartons had been stolen.

In line with industry practice everyone who had anything to do with the container was liable, and this included the sea carrier. The fact that it is difficult to conceive of a theft of this type and size occurring at sea is irrelevant. In denying liability the sea carrier is always in a weak position. Hence, the International Maritime Bureau was asked to investigate. Our thoughts were directed at the alien seal which was identified by the surveyor as TFL 68714. We began the process of tracing it.

Such were conditions in Lebanon at the time that we were unable to contact the surveyor to ascertain seal type. We were starting from scratch. Since we maintain records of all seal manufacturers we sent out a circular requesting details of seal TFL 68714. All but one manufacturer replied but none of them was able to help with the identification of the seal. We then tried the alternative approach and attempted to identify TFL. Eventually we identified it as an American company. We found that TFL 68714 had been produced for the company by the one manufacturer who did not reply to our circular. Once the seal had arrived in the USA it was sent on to the company's European operation, in Valencia. This was crucial—we had the seal and the container in the same port.

Our enquiries in Valencia revealed the remainder of the story. In short, after the contents had been checked by customs the wrong seal had been applied. In other words it had been checked intact, it had been properly sealed, albeit with the wrong seal. It was human error. We are led to the conclusion that the consignees, having noticed the wrong seal, seized their opportunity to claim that the goods were missing, and made a fraudulent claim.

In the above case it is difficult to offer crime prevention advice, but more generally there are three main points that I would particularly like to make. The first concerns motivation. It is a truism to say that if things do not alter they will stay as they are. This is so with cargo crime. As long as the industry can live with the problem as it is then there will be no move to change things. It is true to say that, although there are some large and spectacular crimes, the total loss figure is very small, at least compared with the total throughput of containers. Thus those who end up footing the bill—the insurers or others where liability is established—can afford the present level of crime. There is no financial motive which could provide the catalyst for improvement.

The second point is operational. Many of the problems of container security have their origins in the short-sightedness of those who tried to adapt a conventional cargo checking and liability system to the modern container system. This clearly has not worked. We need to start afresh—but of course that will never happen.

The third point concerns the container itself. With the benefit of hindsight it was unwise to make the sealing system part of the locking mechanism; it should have been totally independent. Eventually as containers are replaced or redesigned this may happen. But for such changes to make a real impact the improvement would need to be considerable.

Discussion

Q. It strikes me that your end point is that everyone is happy. I mean the thief is happy because he is getting away with the stuff. The insurance companies are not concerned because they are not losing too much, the police don't want to deal with the people out there on the ocean because they would rather deal with people who have been burgled and people who drop litter and things. We haven't really got a problem here. Perhaps the answer is that everyone is happy.

A. Nobody is so unhappy that they want to alter the system. When it comes to international commercial crime, police forces, and I will have to generalise, have an incompetence that is imposed upon them. The police have finite resources and they appear to have infinite problems at the moment. Therefore, politically and operationally they are given a pecking order, and international commercial crime, whether it be theft or fraud which Eric Ellen was discussing earlier, is low down in the order of priorities. The only sanction that exists against the international fraudster is the possibility that he might not get away with it; yet very few are caught and prosecuted. I can give you hundreds of examples where law enforcement has been either unwilling or unable to take an interest. In some of the countries where you have commercial problems, the expertise of the police in those areas is limited to a club and a gun. Other than that there is nothing. But if you have an international problem, don't think the police at the other end are like the British or the Dutch. You are not going to get, generally speaking, a law enforcement response to your international commercial problems.

Q. Given what you have said would we not be better advised, at least from a security point of view, to get rid of containers and go back to the old system?

A. The short answer is 'no'. It is important to remember that for every container that is attacked there are probably a thousand, if not more, which arrive at their destination intact. So with everything in perspective, the commercial advantages accruing to the majority more than compensate for the occasional unfortunate experience of a minority.

Q. You mentioned at the end of your paper that the security seal should be independent of the locking system. Is this happening? Do others involved agree that this offers the most positive way forward?

A. Yes, there is a device recently produced which is attached to the lower end of one of the locking bars, and this goes some way to meeting the need. However, it stands scant chance of commercial success because there is little motivation for containers to be modified to incorporate such a device. First, it costs money and no-one will use it unless they can see a good return on their investment. Second, crime affects comparatively few and hence there is no grassroots enthusiasm to urge the manufacturers and carriers to adopt the system.

HM Customs and maritime crime

Paul Devlin and Robin Cooper

Despite the immense growth in air traffic, smuggling by sea has remained a major problem. The days of chasing the Parson's brandy and the Clerk's baccy are, thankfully, gone, although 'beer runners' and tobacco traffickers, exploiting Single Market rules, are causing a new problem. For HM Customs though the priorities today are illicit drugs, weapons, and a variety of other prohibited and restricted goods.

Our maritime role can be summarised as follows: we provide a mobile, flexible seaborne force capable of maintaining an effective deterrent against drug trafficking and other offences both within and outside the territorial waters of the UK. Our role is changing from a static to a non-static one. We are now adopting a proactive role in the fight against crime, working in co-operation with national and international associations and groups. The purpose of this paper is to outline our role, looking in more detail at our partnership approach, and as an example, our drugs work. Given that these days it is a requirement for all businesses, and this includes official bodies, to show they are effective, we shall make some comments on the extent to which we believe we are achieving our objectives.

Organisation

At the forefront of our maritime strategy is the Department's Marine Branch which controls and co-ordinates our fleet of cutters. These are used in joint operations with 14 regions across the UK, with our specialist Investigation Division and with other national and international enforcement agencies. The fleet currently consists of seven ocean-going cutters and over 70 smaller craft used for inshore and harbour work. We are very keen to take a proactive stance these days; our role as static Customs controls is a thing of the past.

The importance of maintaining our boats, with their sophisticated surveillance and communications equipment, is self-evident in a country as geographically vulnerable to seaborne smuggling as the UK. While most innocent travellers have felt the familiar tingle of nervousness when passing through conventional Customs controls, what better way for the guilty to avoid the experience than to use a remote beach or harbour, skipping around fixed controls altogether?

Our cutters and officers are unarmed, which is not always the case with our adversaries. While we can, if necessary, call upon the assistance of the Armed Forces and armed police, we prefer the weapons of intelligence, advanced technology and experience. We are aided by a robust and comprehensive set of laws:

> Where any ship liable to forfeiture or examination as aforesaid has failed to bring to when required to do so and chase has been given thereto by any vessel in the service of Her Majesty and, after the commander of that vessel has hoisted the proper ensign and caused a gun to be fired as a signal, the ship may be fired upon.
>
> *Customs and Excise Management Act* 1979 (Section 91 (2))

Fortunately, we rarely have to use our more draconian powers.

It is the Commissioners of HM Customs and Excise who determine through the system of 'approved wharves' where goods may be loaded or unloaded and under what conditions those operations may be carried out. To avoid goods that have not been entered 'leapfrogging' along the coastline, we also have authority to control the operations of coastwise traffic. We have a long record of success in preventing evasion of customs and excise duties and other commercial dues associated with maritime trade. Much of our work depends on co-operation with other agencies and the general public, and here we have made considerable progress.

Collaboration

Where necessary, we intercept vessels in territorial or international waters, either on our own initiative or at the request of another state under the powers given by the Criminal Justice (International Co-operation) Act of 1990. We also cooperate with other European Union states, the Channel Islands and the Isle of Man. In a different way we help enforce the Misuse of Drugs Act of 1971 on behalf of the Home Office. The concise and clear terms of Section 3 (1) of that Act form a central foundation of our modern day activities. It states simply that:

(a) the importation of a controlled drug; and
(b) the exportation of a controlled drug, are hereby prohibited.

A breach of that section is what is commonly referred to as drug smuggling—the detection, investigation and prosecution of the offence being assigned to Customs under the provisions of the Customs and Excise Management Act of 1979.

In fulfilling our role, we are frequently involved in joint exercises and operations with other member states of the European Union, closely monitoring and inspecting yachts and other light pleasure craft. Working in liaison with our land-based colleagues, especially mobile intelligence units, our maritime role is increasingly focusing on the threat posed by rigid and semi-rigid inflatable fast boats which cross the Channel directly from the continent. These small fast craft are particularly favoured for running cannabis, amphetamines and 'ecstasy' from the Belgian and Dutch coast on to Britain's many empty beaches and into remote anchorages and estuaries. We also co-operate closely with the Ministry of Defence where specialist resources are required.

In many ways partnership and co-operation have become the leitmotif of our organisation. This strategy involves many other services and sectors including the police and the commercial world where information sharing can raise the level of intelligence. It is worth commenting on each of these.

Police and Customs fulfil different roles but aim at a common goal. Crossover is inevitable and results in frequent joint operations and both formal and ad hoc co-operation at all levels. We share intelligence through the National Criminal Intelligence Service staffed jointly by police and customs officers. In terms of the commercial sector, the UK has signed over 40 memoranda of understandings with representatives from the transport industry, both commercial and recreational. By concentrating primarily on the trade associations, the UK now has approximately 10,000 members all committed to helping Customs combat smuggling.

Moreover, we have urged our counterparts around the world to adopt similar co-operative practices and the UK has secured the adoption of a United Nation's resolution promoting our stance. We also help major trade and shipping groups, port authorities and other representative groupings to identify risks. They pass on information about matters of interest, such as proposed uneconomic loads or unexpected arrivals. Access to databases containing details of loads, tickets, routes, etc.—which can be analysed in confidence—can help to target illicit activity. This is a useful counterbalance to the removal of our formal visible presence in the Single Market era. It enables us to take away more of the red tape of formalities that used to inhibit the free movement of innocent trade. By co-operating with the trade we can more easily identify 'innocent' movements and the bona fide traveller or transporter is now more likely than ever to pass directly through the port or airport without ever noticing a customs officer let alone being stopped or examined.

We are constantly extending the base of our co-operative pyramid. We have had very useful assistance from members of the general public, both through the free and confidential 'Drug Smuggling Action Line' (a free service allowing the public to telephone Customs in confidence, to report their suspicions), or through organised local projects such as our 'Coastwatch' which operates in the South East of the country. This is based in Dover, Kent, and encourages local people to note the unusual, especially movements of people along the 100 miles of coast for which Dover Customs are responsible. It channels natural curiosity to a useful purpose, at the same time filling any void on the coast. Through these initiatives we can be seen to be active, and at the same time they encourage the public to be more aware of their own role.

The process of transforming the public perception of the customs officer from a buttress in a wall that has to breached on every return trip from holidays, to a protector of society whom we all wish to help will continue to require time, resources and patience. It will of course be worth every penny spent. Armed with the extra eyes and ears which the trade, the public and other agencies have given us, the message will get across to the criminal that, as the title of the BBC television series on our Department said, we are 'Watching You'. Nowhere is this more important than in the fight against drugs.

Drugs

Our Management Plan sets out our priorities in each area of the Department's business. In the Customs field, our main priority is defined as being to 'fight drug trafficking and enforce import and export prohibitions and restrictions such as those imposed to prevent the spread of weapons of mass destruction'. It is not by accident that drug trafficking is cited first (though our commitment to fight other threats to society is by no means pushed on to a back burner, as witnessed by recent dramatic successes in intercepting terrorist cargoes). Our commitment to combat this threat to society is absolute and needs to be. The United Kingdom continues to be closely targeted by drug smuggling organisations as they scan the world markets in search of greater profits—the sole motive behind drug smuggling whether as an end in itself or to finance other major crime, such as terrorism. The global nature of the trade in illicit drugs has led to their being traded like any other lucrative commodity. The only difference is their illicit nature. Markets are researched, goods are stockpiled to raise the commodity price, released on to the streets in controlled stages and transport is very carefully arranged.

Production and distribution are subject, as with any other naturally produced commodity, to the vagaries of supply and demand, growing seasons, transport difficulties and the availability of reliable routes. The saturation of the North American market for cocaine has led to increased volumes hitting the European market and there is evidence that it is now being 'swapped' for heroin which currently fetches a higher price in the United States. We have seen proof of the move to Europe in recent years in the form of seizures on a scale which would once have been thought impossible here. Since the start of 1992, we have had two well publicised seizures of cocaine, each of which was not far off one tonne in weight. To give some idea of what that represents in monetary terms, imagine a sachet of sugar such as you may have put in your coffee this morning. It probably contained about three grams of white crystals. If they had been of pure cocaine, they would have been worth up to £600 at street level. Scale that up to a 1 kilo bag and the value rises to £200,000. At the one tonne level, the vessel which is necessary to move the goods becomes quite expendable once the deed is done.

Heroin is, if anything, a more valuable product. International conflict has led in the past to population migration in which the refugees have brought their wealth out of affected zones in the form of this powder. Today, the continuing strife in the former Yugoslavia has disrupted the heroin traffickers' favoured 'Balkan Route' and hence they have looked to new ways of reaching the UK. Similarly, the break-up of the former Soviet bloc has created a serious increase in entrepreneurial criminal groups well supplied with commodities for the illegal drugs and arms trades. Ever conscious of a niche in the market, these organisations are not slow to fill a hole in the chain of supply caused by Customs successes. We equally appreciate that the job only begins with the finding of the goods—the follow-up includes looking at who might be tempted to move into the void. Indeed, we are making determined efforts to ensure that we evaluate our effectiveness realistically.

Effectiveness

The discovery of the goods is a tangible proof of our effectiveness, and we are constantly seeking ways to improve. If we return momentarily to our kilo bag of powder, the trafficker's key task is to make it the customs officer's needle in a haystack. The bigger the haystack the more difficult the detection. When the haystack is mobile on the open sea, it becomes even more so; space is at a premium for the trafficker. Unlike the genuine traveller or transporter, he is acutely aware of inaccessible and normally unused space. He has an eye open for a cheap reliable 38-tonne lorry or currently unused oil-rig supply vessel and he is willing to pay cash. The development of containerised freight, easily transferred between modes of transport as large, sealed units, has proved a popular means of conveying compact, high-value contraband. The offenders are using their imagination in concealing drugs and other commodities within these containers. Small quantities transported by air, including by internal body concealment, remains a favourite method, notwithstanding the risks run by the couriers. Deep concealments in the bodywork of heavy goods vehicles from the Near East are regularly detected at the ferry ports. Whereas big consignments were previously the preserve of the cannabis smuggler who dealt in a high-bulk and lower-value commodity, the trafficker in hard drugs has now followed suit.

In our strategy we have no wish or need to examine every movement of goods. The often mooted 'fortress Europe' or 'fortress Britain', even if we were able to achieve it, would not be a practical solution. Just as the educator abides by the governing precepts of the 'three R's', today's customs officer adheres to our version—Risk, Resource and Results. Prioritisation of effort is undertaken by extensive risk assessment. This is not only based on previous experience, but draws upon the intelligence gathered by our own staff, members of the Anti-Drug Alliance, the public, and also on technical research into trends and results analysis.

This assessment produces precisely drawn profiles which assist our officers in target selection. They are not rigid and are constantly tested and updated—too strict an adherence to one profile would quickly lead the trafficker to work outside it. We concentrate much of our resources at natural 'pinch points' where experience shows that they will deliver against targets and we have a large proportion of mobile officers who can move where demand leads, and here, of course, our Marine Branch is custom-built for efficiency.

We have to operate on business-like lines. This means validating our activities. The success or otherwise of the assessment and resource allocation will be gauged against specific targets, particularly our Drugs Key Result Area. This is not a crystal ball exercise for the forthcoming year but a measure used to determine the effect of our anti-drugs efforts. It goes beyond the simple measurement of the amount or value of drugs seized to calculate the effect of our performance during the year in question on the UK drugs market; it seeks to project and express in monetary terms the amount of drugs which were prevented from entering the country. This is done by adding a qualitative element, namely the effect of our interceptions on smuggling organisations. By setting ourselves a target based on the previous year's performance, we give ourselves a real and challenging task and a regular snapshot of how we are performing.

The process of knowing your opposition, allocating resources to deal with it, training those resources and informing them through co-operation inside and outside HM Customs is a demanding one. When it all 'clicks' and produces a smooth operation, the result is frequently spectacular. A classic example which occurred in late 1988 will serve to illustrate the point. The vessel *Salton Sea* was intercepted in the English Channel. This 190 tonnes Honduran registered cargo vessel was challenged by the French cutter *Vent d'Aval* in the Channel and chase was given. Shots were fired across her bows. She was shepherded into the port of Ramsgate by the HM Customs and Excise cutter *Swift* and detained. There followed a deep rummage, which included specialist units—drug dog teams and divers. Following the discovery of small amounts of cocaine in the deck area and cannabis in the cabins, a large deep concealment was discovered in the hull, which proved to contain over 10 tonnes of herbal cannabis. The vessel was seized as forfeit to the Crown. Without slicing it apart like some vast steel salami, we could not be sure that all of the contraband had been recovered. We had reason to believe that other drugs might be concealed in its structure, so it did not follow the normal path of seized vessels—sale by private tender. After the engines were removed and sold, we passed it to the Royal Navy for target practice and it was dispatched to Davy Jones's locker. Title remained with the Commissioners of Customs and Excise, so this is the only recorded example of the Navy deliberately sinking a Customs owned vessel.

Summary

It has not been possible to detail all our work or our successes. We have said very little about our attempts to control the illegal flow of weapons. Well publicised cases here include the shipload of terrorist weapons bound for Northern Ireland which we intercepted in co-operation with the Polish authorities. Following the break-up of the former Soviet bloc, increasing volumes of weapons are becoming available for illicit purposes. To this problem is added the more routine Customs role of preventing the entry of items freely available elsewhere—CS gas canisters, stun guns, flick knives and a host of other controlled items.

We hope it will be clear that the role of HM Customs today is very different from yesteryear. The changes that have taken place have provided new opportunities. As offenders, and especially smugglers, have become more sophisticated so the agencies charged with countering the threat have had to develop their expertise. We cannot claim infallibility, nor are we complacent, but we are confident that our systems are well geared up to dealing with the threat that is posed. We are improving but we are always looking for ways of doing better.

Discussion

Q. HM Customs appears to be expanding rapidly: is this expansion being accompanied by increased resources?

A. Customs and Excise as a Department is not expanding. As a result of our Fundamental Expenditure Review which builds upon changes in operational techniques (including the use of better targeted, intelligence led, flexible interceptions in place of static routine checks) we shall take out a little under 300 posts from static controls. However, we shall add 50 posts into intelligence led investigation in the next two financial years. We shall carefully assess the impact of these changes to check overall effectiveness has been improved.

Q. Do all other countries have Customs departments similar to this country? Is it easy to collaborate with other Customs departments?

A. Co-operation with partners in the European Union, both at a policy and operational level, is well established and works well. The global nature of the illicit drugs trade means that the breaking up of trafficking organisations can entail complex operations involving a number of Customs authorities. They also exchange views and information bilaterally and through our umbrella organisation, the Customs Co-operation Council (CCC) which has over 130 members. Differences in national laws, attitudes and problems mean that individual customs services may have different resources, methods and priorities.

Q. Are you involved in investigating or preventing thefts of boats since this is where most maritime crime, and particularly smuggling offences, begins?

A. Theft is not an assigned matter and we are not actively involved in preventing or investigating it. However, we do in the course of our activities come across many stolen articles including stolen means of transport. Having established what facts we can, we then hand the theft aspect of the case over to the police. A typical example is where during the holiday season we might examine movements of vehicles returning from the continent and notice cars which left the country unaccompanied, and return towing caravans. Given that the police work closely with us at ports and airports and that we have excellent co-operation, these cases can be smoothly handed over.

Q. A very simple question really—do we have smuggling under control?

A. That is a far from simple question—in fact, a very difficult one—the great imponderable. When seizure totals for the year show an increase should we be content that we are seizing more of what is being smuggled, or concerned because there is more of it about? In order to be able to make a judgement one needs to know the totality of what is available to be smuggled—the size of the whole clandestine market. That cannot be known. It is for this reason that Customs have never claimed to be winning or to have the situation under control. It is also for this reason that we never give a figure for a proportion that we catch. Any pundit who gives such a figure must be taken with a large pinch of salt, for it is pure speculation. Of course we will try to gauge our effectiveness, but we have to use indicators which are not based on any indication of the market size—it is for that reason that our Key Result Area is based on a measurable criterion—what we prevent from entering the country.

Q. You mentioned that you collaborate with the commercial world. Could you expand on this a little; for example, how does this work? Do they pay for information and advice or what?

A. We collaborate with the commercial sector principally through the Anti-Drugs Alliance. Responsibility for liaising with and educating our Memorandum of Understanding co-signatories lies with Memorandum of Understanding liaison officers who are located throughout the country. Through presentations, meetings, seminars and training courses they will advise companies on how to improve security to reduce the risk of their transport, premises or staff being used for trafficking. We also use their staff as our additional eyes and ears. They are kept up to date by means of a newsletter. This is not done for payment—the gains are that we in Customs get to identify high risk traffic, and the genuine trade receives protection and can flow more easily.

Q. How have staff adjusted to the change of role you outlined? I am thinking here of the move from a static to a non-static response. It sounds much more exciting.

A. The move away from static controls was not an overnight affair and staff have had the opportunity to adapt. The prime engines for change in this area were internal reviews and the arrival of the Single Market.

We were ahead of the market in both aspects—we have always had some mobile units and the changes to our anti-smuggling methods were based on a degree of experience. There was also the recognition that effectiveness would increase if we moved to a greater concentration on intelligence and had less of a tendency to wait for the mountain to come to Mohammed. Generally, the change in style has been welcomed. It has also brought with it a more competitive edge, with staff knowing they are expected to use their mobility to come up with results.

Maritime crime and prevention—a police perspective

John Wilks

Being a constable who has served for the last 24 years with the Essex Police Marine Unit on the River Thames, I am probably one of the longest serving marine police officers in the country. During that time I have specialised in marine crime prevention and boat security as a service for an identified section of the community, the leisure boat industry.

In bringing a police perspective to marine crime in Essex we need to begin with a few basic details about the county. The coastline of Essex, if we include the banks of the rivers in the county, is about 250 miles long. In fact the county is bounded on three sides by water—the North Sea, the Thames and Blackwater estuaries to the east, the River Thames to the south and the River Lee to the west. There is also the River Stour in the north although most of this river is non-navigable, and the River Lee which is non-tidal and does not occupy us greatly.

However, the three main rivers (the Thames, the Blackwater and the Crouch), and many of the secondary ones and backwaters are all extensively used by the leisure boating public. Most have good deep-water mooring facilities backed up by marinas. There are also berths offered by private companies as well as mud berths (the main exception to this being the Thames). The coast and the rivers are all shallow in a nautical sense with sand banks in evidence some 12 miles from shore. Although these present navigational hazards in their own right, they also result in the rivers being considered safe havens for the boating public. Consequently the boat population is high. Many of those involved come from outside the county, including the Midlands and the North West.

So our problems are that we have numerous boats in all kinds of remote areas; that they are accessible from the shore, especially at low water; and that owners live anywhere from across the road to 300 miles away. The obvious way forward would be to build more marinas but there just isn't the capital to make that a viable proposition.

So what has been the police response? The Essex Police Marine Unit is divided into two sections, one based at Rayleigh near to Southend and the other at Burnham-on-Crouch. The Unit is headed by an inspector who is also head of the Essex Police Air Support Unit. As a consequence we have been able to develop the use of aircraft to supplement and assist with marine patrols.

I shall be referring specifically to the Rayleigh section where I am based, and any statistics can be doubled to give approximate figures for the county as a whole. Our section was set up in 1949, and worked from Tilbury with the somewhat ambitious remit of policing commercial shipping. Over time, and particularly from the mid-1970s, it became increasingly obvious that our principal interests lay with leisure boating. Marine crime was on the increase and it was being fuelled by the increasing number of private boats moving into, and passing through, our area. We discovered very quickly that the characteristics of the leisure boat industry were not such as to help us in our role as police officers. Boats were not registered, and serial numbers relating to boat equipment were rarely recorded. Hence, while outboard engines, echo sounders and marine VHF radios were popular targets for thieves, there was very little chance of their being recovered.

In those early days it was clear to us that the way forward in policing was tied up with the development of a register for boats. The only one existing at that time was based in Cardiff and was concerned with vessels registered at an acknowledged port. The process of getting boats registered was a lengthy and expensive one, usually pursued by the more wealthy owners often as a status symbol.

In 1977 we decided, as an experiment, to organise our own register. We started by approaching our local yacht club and asked if they would like to participate. Initially they were sceptical; I recall they were troubled by the twin concerns of a potential infringement of their liberty and what they feared was the beginnings of bureaucracy. They required assurances and we outlined our plans—all personal details would be used by us only and not given over to routine checks of criminal records. Moreover, we had to persuade them that it would be in their own interests if we were to have available details of the boat, the owner, the serial numbers and types of equipment on board, the location of the mooring and the names of persons who had access to the boat. Then if we found the boat adrift, or insecure, or in the possession of suspicious character we would be able to quickly identify the owner and establish the facts. The club decided to go along with the idea and by the end of the first year 80 per cent of its members were registered.

At the end of 1978 the Unit was moved from Tilbury to its current base in Rayleigh. The move interrupted development of the scheme, but in 1980 we began trying to extend registration to other clubs. The response was poor: no more than a quarter of club members and a few non-members were joining. We needed help and it came in the form of the Southend Crime Prevention Panel. They provided some money for a pamphlet to promote crime prevention ideas for boat owners. We included a page on the registration scheme, and in collaboration with alarm and lock companies we circulated ideas on physical crime prevention.

Elsewhere there were moves to encourage registration. Prompted by the requirement to show proof of ownership when taking a vessel to France, the Royal Yachting Association (RYA) were authorised to set up a system of registration. They issued a registration number which was prefixed by the letters SSR (Small Ships Register). Unfortunately there was a big problem; the system operated by the RYA did not demand proof of ownership from the people registering. This problem was highlighted for me several years ago when I was involved in the investigation of a theft of a Halberg Rassy yacht from Stockholm. It was eventually traced and recovered in Middleberg, Holland. I discovered that it had been in the possession of a man from Britain who had changed its name and registered it with the SSR, and then withdrawn it a month later, all by letter. Not only did he not have to provide proof of ownership, he did not need to provide any proof of identity. The system has now been taken over by the Driver Vehicle Licensing Centre at Swansea, although it is to be put up for tender every few years and its future is uncertain.

This development made it more difficult to persuade boat owners to register their boats with us. We maintained our active approach but the involvement of club members settled around the 22 per cent mark. Also, by now changes in ownership were occurring, details of which were not being forwarded to us. The only way our register was going to survive was for us to be persistent.

Things took a rather different turn in the mid-1980s when a new buzz term arrived from America—neighbourhood watch. The system, as I am sure most will be aware, is based on the idea of neighbours joining together to watch over each others' property. The neighbours appoint a co-ordinator and through him/her information regarding anyone or anything of a suspicious nature is passed on to the local beat officer. At the outset, senior officers were keen to ensure that these schemes were set up in collaboration with the police to ensure that vigilantism did not gain a hold.

We in the marine section were keen to pick up on the idea. We had been pushing the idea of property marking for some time, and now that this was part of the national neighbourhood watch initiative we had another opportunity to promote our ideas. We contacted our local chandlers, boat builders, and insurance brokers to promote property marking kits. These kits are briefcases containing ultra violet pens, an electric engraver, hand scribes and dyes in letters and numerals. Instructions and postal code books are also included. We sensed we could make an impact.

Initially we worked with crime prevention officers, but we soon decided to take the initiative ourselves. We produced a folder full of marine crime prevention information. This includes a booklet, a registration card, a Home Office pamphlet on protecting boats, incident report cards encouraging boat owners to report anything suspicious and stickers to identify them as members of what we called 'marine watch'.

We saw the incident report cards as a potential generator of information about marine crime. We promised anonymity, and an investigation into any incident reported. However, it has not been a success. In eight years I have known only two reports to be returned. Either people cannot be bothered, or they do not want to get involved with the police.

However, simultaneously we had begun to expand our role; the unit started to investigate marine crimes, defined as offences on or immediately adjacent to the water. While, as a police officer, I am only too aware that official statistics only give a partial picture some people may nevertheless be interested in just two observations. In 1989 when marine watch was at its height our biggest category of crime—theft from boats—fell quite markedly. Then in 1992 the overall figures for marine crime fell, no mean achievement given that figures for the force as a whole went up by about 10 per cent. While marine crime is, comparatively, a very small problem, it is ours and we like to think we take it seriously.

Taking the matter seriously is not something insurance companies appear to do. Their attitude puzzles me and I want to use this platform to say something about it. They seem to be only too ready to pay up. Even when they suspect claims have been fraudulent there has frequently been little investigation. It is all too easy; the serial number of a piece of equipment is obtained and then the item is reported as stolen, dropped overboard or lost. The money is paid out in full, and the claimant never even owned the item in the first place. Another example concerns the case of a fisherman who reported that he had found three yachts adrift on the River Thames, their mooring line having been cut. The fisherman salvaged the three yachts and then submitted a claim to the insurance companies for salvage. To the disgust of yacht owners in the marine section who were investigating the incident, the insurance companies paid out almost by return. Had the insurance companies carried out even the most cursory enquiry they would have found that the chief suspect was the fisherman himself. In this case summary justice was meted out by some of his colleagues and there have been no repeat incidents in our area.

My point here is that insurance companies must become more responsible. They must insist that each item of property is associated with a serial number and value on the proposal form. In addition, they should request proof of purchase. This will not solve all the problems but alongside other changes it will help. On the subject of other changes, I would like to draw attention to the potential of two physical devices which are much in evidence. But first, registration schemes.

In 1987, together with other officers from Essex, I attended the Annual Marine Police Conference at New Scotland Yard to provide information on the current Essex situation concerning marine watches and boat registration. We were astonished to find that the Metropolitan Police River Section were using the conference to launch the boat watch scheme. Other marine units were still in the throes of boat registrations. All of these units were at least three years behind Essex, and were still learning about the apathy of the public towards protecting their own equipment. I do not mention this to boast about the work of the Essex Marine Unit, but rather to highlight the fact that there is poor communication on the subject, and that other units could have learned much had they contacted us. These forces thought that the launching of their registration schemes would make things easy. Our experience, and now theirs, have proved them wrong.

I am convinced that it is not so much the police approach to registration that is the problem as an endemic dislike within the marine community of anything that is associated with bureaucracy. Tim Goodhead will pick up on this matter later, but I can point to the failure of a private venture as supporting my case. What I think is agreed, certainly within police circles, is that we need a better way of identifying marine property. With the exception of outboard engines there was no facility for this on the Police National Computer until very recently. Consequently the Association of Chief Police Officers commissioned a private registration database company to undertake this service. However, since it requires boat owners to register their boats for an annual fee, and experience has proved that they will not register their boats even when it is free, I am not optimistic about its potential. Indeed, I have not yet heard of any property being identified through the scheme.

So what about other commercial involvement? I am afraid that again I must run the risk of causing offence, but there are things that need to be said. I am referring to various current ideas which are described as tagging, electronic tagging and electronic marking. Without going into details here the basic idea is that a micro chip or bar code chip is installed in the hull of the boat which can then be read by a tagging gun with details being recorded on a screen. We have identified two problems. First, there are too many schemes on the market, and until one tagging gun can read all the chips we would need a lot of guns. Second, there is the issue of cost. I have been advised by tagging companies that they will sell the chips for about £80 to £100, and that the subscription for the data to be retained will be from £11 to £15 per annum. Having carried out a straw poll at meetings I attended recently when I asked who would be prepared to spend this sort of money on boat security, I found the response to be nil, a 100 per cent negative.

I was recently approached by a company offering the chip and registration for a single payment of £19.95. However, when I enquired further I found that it had encountered problems in America. Apparently, the waving of some magic wand around the perimeter resulted in the chips, tags or bar codes being wiped clean. Until there is a foolproof and economic system there will not be official support.

In conclusion, I must point out that the boating fraternity have been negligent in caring for their property. It amazes me that someone can purchase a £40,000 boat and then march off to buy a padlock for £2.50 to secure it—a padlock that goes rusty in five minutes and can be broken easily with a hammer. For about £40 it is possible to buy a stainless steel padlock with a shank which is difficult to cut with bolt croppers, but people do not seem to be prepared to make the effort. All we can do as police officers is cajole, persuade and educate. Meanwhile, we will continue to implore insurance companies to require more details on proposal forms; we will remain open-minded to ideas from the commercial world; and we will watch and listen carefully to the debates about the merits of compulsory registration.

Discussion

Q. You mentioned the number of boats that have been stolen but then you go on to say these are on the water or adjacent to it. What about all these boats that get stolen from people's drives?

A. That is not our direct responsibility; our brief is crime on or adjacent to the water. We are advised of other marine crimes but realistically it would not be possible to travel all over the county to investigate everything.

Q. Some of what you have said gives a very misleading impression. I am thinking about what you have said about insurance companies not placing enough emphasis on gaining information and so on. We run a big scheme for speed boats and we insist on serial numbers and anti-theft devices. We even check on serial numbers and we check with different groups to ensure serial numbers are right. A lot of us in insurance are trying to prevent theft. I think the impression that is being given is that insurance companies tend to sit back and they are not really bothered as long as they get the premium.

A. Yes, this is a point that I omitted, and one I had intended to make. Over the last two years insurance companies have been taking a far more active role. They are encouraging the use of equipment and anti-theft devices. Some are looking at the sort of equipment that we mentioned, like the tagging devices. Some insurance companies are voiding claims where serial numbers and proof of purchase are not available. Yes, I will accept that some, and that word needs emphasising, are making appropriate efforts.

Q. My impression is that almost every boat that gets stolen is being towed away behind a car. If the police stopped more people towing boats behind cars and asked for identification or proof of identity, and made a note of things on the boat, a lot of thefts could be picked up almost at source. Is this practical?

A. We once tried to launch a scheme with an adjacent force. We devised a form which was to be completed by officers from the traffic department when they stopped cars with trailed boats. The idea was that this information would then be passed to a marine intelligence officer. However, the scheme never materialised, and for several reasons. First, the company sponsoring and supplying the literature went into bankruptcy. Then the marine unit in the adjacent county was disbanded for a period while a review was held about its future, and when it was reinstated it was greatly reduced in size. This resulted in a lack of enthusiasm for the scheme especially since traffic officers are being asked to carry out caravan checks, horse box checks, etc. It has recently been recommenced, but it is too early to judge its effectiveness.

Q. You were talking about the equipment that goes adrift; your force does send us information, that is to the Marine Equipment Register at Holyhead, by fax and on a daily basis. This information is stored in our database. You are quite right about the owners; there is a high degree of

45

apathy about registering equipment. They work on the principle that it is insured so if it gets lost or stolen then it is a problem for their insurance company. We are having a look at the whole system at the moment. There is another point I would just like to comment on. You were saying that we are approved by ACPO and that is correct and we have been for the past three years. We do enjoy a good relationship with all the forces including yourselves. We do get information about stolen equipment on a daily basis, the system does work and would be better if more registered.

A. Yes I know with our own force there is a specific route. It has to go through the Force Information Bureau. They fax all the messages through to you—we are not allowed to do it direct.

Q. If the insurance companies were to exclude the risk of theft would that reduce your figures? You would not get the fraudulent claims.

A. Yes, it is true that we would not get the fraudulent claims, but you must remember there are many genuine claims as well.

Boat owners as crime victims—patterns of victimisation

Martin Gill

Introduction

In recent years criminologists have begun to look at how and why some people are more likely to become crime victims. It is clear that lifestyle, type of job and area of residence are just some of the factors that influence the likelihood of becoming a victim. In a different way it is recognised that while vehicle crime is a growing problem, certain types of vehicles are more at risk than others. However, there have not been any attempts to examine the extent of boat-related crime. While, as will be shown, official statistics do not reflect the extent of maritime crime, alternative methods of measuring crime, for example a crime survey which includes questions about victimisation, have yet to target boat owners specifically. Without a good understanding of why, how and when crime occurs it is difficult to recommend appropriate security measures. This paper is based on a survey of boat owners designed to clarify the extent of their victimisation and their use of and attitudes toward security and crime prevention measures.

The first stage involved writing to all police forces, canal/harbour/port/river authorities, boating and maritime organisations, and other parties to collect details. It was interesting to find that while many were unable to provide anything other than general information there was considerable enthusiasm for the study. Many requested that they be provided with details of the findings.

The second stage was a survey of boat owners. Ideally it would have been desirable to use a national sample. Unfortunately, gaining access to records of boat owners proved difficult. In the event Dorset police and the States of Jersey police agreed to facilitate access to records held by local harbour authorities and these areas were therefore chosen as the focus of the study. In all close to 4,000 boat owners were sent questionnaires and about a third (N = 1,306), a reasonable response rate, provided information. Clearly, this should be borne in mind although the ultimate aim here was to provide a base upon which future research might build.

Findings

Although information was sought from a number of sources, the most comprehensive statistics on theft and criminal damage were provided by the police. While many police forces—following Home Office guidelines—do not use a separate category for recording boat crime, those able to provide details are shown in Table 1. Some areas were unspecific about the types of crime suffered and these have been classified as 'unspecified crime'. There were also local variations in terminology. For example, the category 'Theft from boat' includes thefts both from on deck and by breaking and entering.

There are two particular points of interest here. First, and predictably, there are regional variations. Second, and more importantly, the table clearly demonstrates the limits of the information available. Unless the Home Office redefine the classification system and require forces to record boat crime separately its extent will remain hidden.

However, some police forces were able to indicate the cost of boat-related crime. Lothian and Borders police reported that £2,410 worth of property was stolen as the result of thirteen maritime break-ins and thefts in 1991. The value of goods recovered was only £60. Moreover, five boats, with a value of £43,470, were reported stolen of which two, with a value of £22,300, were recovered. Although Merseyside police were unable to provide statistics they did record the value of property stolen as £71,000 in 1991. Essex police revealed that boat-related crime resulted in losses of £186,000 in 1990/1991. Detailed information was made available by Devon and Cornwall where recorded losses totalled a staggering £724,159. Boat-related crime can quite clearly involve significant financial loss.

A survey of boat owners

The purpose of this survey was to gain an insight into the boat owners' experience of crime. The survey included a range of questions about criminal victimisation (focusing specifically on theft and criminal damage offences). For example, questions were included to identify the most common location for crime, and the types of security measures used. Boat owners were asked about their experience of marking schemes which can assist in the identification of (stolen) property, about boat watch schemes, (a development from neighbourhood watch initiatives), and also about national registers of boat owners which may serve a security function.

Table 1. Police crime statistics 1991 by type of crime

Police area	TOB	TOM	TFT	TFB	CD	U
Avon & Somerset	0	0	0	0	0	106
Bedfordshire	0	0	0	0	0	112
Central Scotland	24	37	4	14	0	0
Cheshire	4	0	0	41	0	0
Cleveland[6]	1	0	0	3	0	0
Devon & Cornwall	378	416	6	16	1	0
Dorset	33	57	0	122	0	431
Dover Harbour Board	0	0	0	0	0	6
Dumfries & Galloway	14	14	0	26	0	0
Essex	41	35	0	125	39	0
Grampian	0	0	0	174	0	0
Humberside	44	0	0	57	0	0
Isle of Man	3	0	0	11	0	0
States of Jersey	30	0	0	0	13	4
Kent	135	0	0	0	0	0
Lincolnshire	0	0	0	0	0	25
Lothian & Borders	5	0	0	13	0	0
Metropolitan (Thames)	0	0	0	0	0	194
Northumbria[6]	0	0	0	0	0	477
Royal Ulster	0	0	0	117	5	0
Strathclyde	0	0	0	0	0	258
Suffolk	50	0	0	0	0	0
Sussex	3	2	0	3	0	0
Thames	79	0	0	0	0	0
West Mercia	28	0	0	57	0	0
Wiltshire	21	0	2	1	0	0
Totals	893	561	12	780	58	1,613

TOB = Theft of boat
TOM = Theft of outboard motor
TFT = Theft from trailer
TFB = Theft from boat
CD   = Criminal damage
U   = Unspecified crime

[6] These statistics relate to 1990 and 1991

Of the 1,306 questionnaires returned, 739 (56.7 per cent) were from Jersey, 495 (38 per cent) from Dorset, while 72 (5.5 per cent) did not specify and they have been classified as 'other'. The vast majority of respondents, 1,404 (92.7 per cent), claimed to own their boat for pleasure purposes, the remainder noted that they used their boat for business purposes (including some of those who owned a fishing boat) or a combination of business and pleasure purposes.

It was instructive to find that criminal victimisation varied with the type of boat owned. About three in ten power boat owners reported being victims of some sort of crime, but it was nearer four in ten for owners of cabin cruisers, and more than this for owners of yachts and boats with outboard motors. The most victimised were owners of fishing boats and dinghies more than five in ten of whom reported some type of crime in the previous three years (none of the owners of jet skis reported being victims).

Further analysis showed that most crime reported was against yachts, but there were more of them. Proportionally fishing boat owners were more susceptible to theft of equipment—this was mentioned by a quarter. However, this was also true for a fifth of owners of powerboats, a sixth of boats with outboard motors, and a seventh of cabin cruisers and yachts. Indeed, it appeared that equipment was the most likely target for thieves, particularly in Dorset where 22 per cent of owners compared with 13.3 per cent in Jersey claimed to have suffered this type of theft at least once in the previous three years. Although fishing boat owners suffered from theft they were the least likely to report being victims of vandalism. Indeed, nobody owning a fishing boat reported an incident of criminal damage. Vandals, it seems, tend to attack cabin cruisers and dinghies.

By far the majority of reported theft and criminal damage offences occurred in harbours, but the sample included a high number of vessels normally moored here. More detailed analysis revealed that river and canal moorings and boatyards were proportionally more prone to suffer crime. Indeed, respondents reported more than one incident per boat for vessels moored in either of these two locations. The next most common mooring for crime was coastal areas where approximately two thirds of owners reported an incident. About half the boats in harbours suffered an incident and about a third of the boats normally moored in marinas. The safest place to keep a boat is at home (including garages and lock ups): little more than a tenth of boat owners who normally kept boats here reported incidents.

Crimes that occurred tended to happen at the normal mooring. This is an important finding because it suggests that effective security here could significantly reduce the number of incidents. In the survey questions covered the types of security measured applied at different moorings. Respondents were asked whether any of the following were present at the place the boat was normally moored: security staff, staffed gates, unstaffed gates, a magnetic PIN gate entry system and security cameras.

The findings were interesting and tended to confirm what might have been expected from the above findings on patterns of victimisation. For example, at coastal moorings there were only seven references to any of the stated security measures. Of boatyards and river/canal moorings about half had one of the stated security measures. About a fifth of boatyards and a third of river/canal moorings recorded the presence of security staff[7]. However, whereas little else was evident at river/canal moorings, another fifth of owners with boats normally moored at boatyards noted the existence of gates (similar proportions noted staffed and unstaffed gates). It has already been reported that most crime occurs in harbours. Only 6.4 per cent of owners of boats normally moored in harbours referred to the presence of security staff and another 3.4 per cent mentioned gates.

Security at all these moorings is by any measure negligible. Indeed, some respondents noted that there was a complete absence of security, and clearly this provides opportunities for crime. What is needed is a security device or procedure capable of protecting vessels in isolated areas such as moorings at rivers, canals and coastal areas. It was noted earlier that less crime occurs in marinas, and it is striking that there were more references to security measures here than at any of the other locations. A little more than six in ten of owners with boats normally moored in marinas indicated the presence of security staff, and over three in ten noted gates which more often than not were said to be staffed. Less than one in ten noted a magnetic PIN entrance system. It was only in the context of marinas that security cameras were evident to any significant extent; they were mentioned by more than three in ten.

In the survey, general questions were asked about the use of padlocks, surface/mortise locks, immobilisers, outboard engine locks and alarms. It was striking that many boat owners did not use security devices of any kind. Only padlocks were used by the majority and, perhaps not surprisingly, they did not prevent theft (and the extent to which they may have reduced it was beyond the scope of this project). In all, more than six in ten owners who mentioned a theft claimed that the item stolen was protected by a padlock.

---

[7] We did not collect information on the type of security staff employed and the duration of cover; that was beyond the scope of this small scale enquiry. However, it may usefully be incorporated in more focused projects.

The survey did not ask for details about the quality of devices. However, the responses on security leave one in little doubt that in terms of protecting their property from crime boat owners were negligent. Protecting boats from crime was clearly viewed as a low priority.

There is at least one rational argument for this attitude. Some argued that because boats were normally moored in isolated areas, or at least at moorings which were generally quiet and unobserved, their vessels were always vulnerable. Extra security would merely increase the amount of damage an offender would do to gain access. During the research it was discovered that in one Scottish boatyard owners were concerned that attacks were being made on their boats by people looking for first aid boxes which sometimes contained drugs. They found that the thieves were persistent and sometimes caused considerable damage to gain access to vessels. They decided that rather than increase the physical security measures they would make access easier (to avoid damage) but remove the target; they took the first aid boxes home and 'made this known locally'. The worry, of course, was that the owners would forget to return the boxes and that medication would not be available when it was needed. During the research, it emerged that similar circumstances had arisen in relation to life rafts.

Boat-related marking schemes are a type of security measure that is becoming more common. This is where codes are marked on vessels and equipment, and information is stored on a central database. This is supposed to operate in the same way as the Driver Vehicle Licence Agency system operates for cars. Unfortunately, there is a gap between theory and practice. One reason is that there are several schemes in operation. Indeed, during the research details were obtained of four schemes. All four retained details on a database which the police could access; three provided a 24-hour hot line; while one claimed to be the only nationally operating database, at least one of the others operated on a national scale too; at least two of the schemes claimed to provide an up to the minute list of stolen vessels and equipment; each company practised a different marking system; the cost of marking and registration in each scheme varied from about £10 to £30 (in 1991) The situation is somewhat confusing.

A second problem, and perhaps a consequence of the first, is that there has been a low take-up. In the survey, only 38 (2.9 per cent) stated that they were members of a marking scheme, and of the 31 who went on to give further details 28 mentioned that the scheme was operated by the police. There were area differences here. Only five (0.7 per cent) in Jersey were members of such a scheme, which is low compared with the 26 (5.3 per cent) in Dorset and seven (10 per cent) in the other category. The small figures limit the scope for analysis, and in any event the survey did not attempt to identify the point at which an owner joined a marking scheme, or more specifically, whether he or she joined after a crime has been committed.

The low numbers involved in marking schemes was in contrast to the majority (74.1 per cent) who claimed that their boat was marked or engraved in some way. Vessels were normally marked by a stick-on or screw-on plate, but some were engraved or chemically etched. Respondents went on to give details of 980 boats, of which the majority 56.3 per cent (552) were marked in more than one place. Of the 37 (91.9 per cent) who reported having a vessel stolen most noted that it was marked. Since details were not asked of when the marking took place this may have happened after a crime, so this finding should not be seen as an indication of their effectiveness. What is most obvious about marking schemes is that they have yet to attract wide support from owners who have not, for the most part, been able to see crime prevention advantages in joining. Their ultimate success in attracting owners may depend on their ability to demonstrate such advantages here.

Some marking schemes are linked to registers. A national or international register of all boats could play an important role in crime prevention and not least in the return of stolen property. However, this has been resisted by the boat-owning fraternity at least in part because of the belief that a register could later facilitate the introduction of a tax. In the survey a number of general questions were asked about the use of registers and attitudes toward registration.

A minority of respondents said they were members of the Merchant Shipping Register (14.7 per cent) and the Small Ships Register (38 per cent) and their reasons for joining were mostly linked to legal requirements. Amongst those not registered three explanations were common: respondents never left the UK, they were unaware of the schemes, or they had never given the matter consideration. Overall, there was no strong resistance to these registers in principle (although only 22 per cent of members claimed registration was 'very useful'). Indeed, when owners were asked whether national registration would be a good idea, about two-thirds replied affirmatively.

Thus, while membership of present registration schemes is not viewed especially favourably, the majority of respondents (with only about a sixth against) favoured a national registration scheme. There are then grounds for suggesting that the scepticism of official bodies to this measure may not represent the views of most boat owners. However, further research needs to be done since the questionnaire did not detail the advantages and disadvantages of such an initiative.

Security procedures are employed not only to prevent crime (or to make it more difficult), but in some cases to assist in the recovery of goods. Unfortunately figures were too small to judge the advantages of different measures in this respect. The vast majority of respondents who reported items stolen added that these were not recovered. This was less the case for owners of stolen dinghies (49.2 per cent) than for those who had outboard motors (24.6 per cent), trailers (6.7 per cent) or equipment (6.4 per cent) taken.

While little is known about marking schemes, watch schemes of various descriptions have become a common feature of British life. In all, 108 (8.3 per cent) respondents stated that they were members of a boat watch scheme. Boat watch schemes were particularly common in harbours, although nearly a fifth of those who said their boat was moored on private premises claimed to be members, suggesting an overlap with neighbourhood or home watch schemes. Respondents were asked to assess the usefulness of the scheme in terms of reducing theft, increasing security, facilitating exchange of information, and providing peace of mind. Each category was ticked by about half the scheme members although a few did not register a view and 21 respondents, that is nearly a fifth, ticked the answer 'not useful'.

In all the categories of theft and vandalism analysed, boat watch members were less likely than non-members to report being victimised. Differences were most marked in the case of theft of equipment where 2.5 per cent of boat watch members against 15.4 per cent of non-members reported this type of crime. Again caution is needed here because of the small figures involved, and because there was no attempt to monitor displacement effects. Future research might usefully develop this aspect.

Most had their boat (1,208, 92.4 per cent) and equipment (1,089 or 83.3 per cent) insured.[8] However, most victims of crime did not make an insurance claim. While more than seven in ten victims of motor thefts did so, only four in ten owners of stolen vessels and dinghies and less than three in ten owners of other types of vessels submitted an insurance claim following an incident. Overall there appeared to be a reluctance to take formal action. Less than half informed the police—which justifies scepticism over official

---

[8] Those who owned boats for pleasure were more likely to have their equipment insured (83.9 per cent) than those who kept a boat for business (75 per cent) or business and pleasure (76.1 per cent). These differences were not apparent for boat insurance.

statistics. Many, including a third of boat owners who reported equipment stolen, admitted that they did nothing at all. Reasons for such apathy were beyond the scope of this enquiry.

Summary

Initially statistical and other information was collated from a variety of official sources, particularly the police. This exercise was instructive, if disappointing. On the one hand it confirmed that the way police statistics are compiled, following Home Office guidelines, neatly obscures the extent of maritime crime. Moreover, even where police areas make attempts to record marine crime independently there is no consistency in the categories used. The survey findings show that this problem is further compounded because as many as half of boat owners who were crime victims did not report the offence to the police. Hence, in drawing attention to the need to alter official recording practices to identify more accurately the extent and patterns of this type of crime, one needs to add that even then this will provide only a partial representation of the extent of the problem. Further research is needed to establish why many victims do not either report the matter to the police or submit an insurance claim.

In all, a significant minority of boat owners had been crime victims; but the findings suggest that not all owners are at equal risk. Most crime was against yachts but there were more of them; fishing boats were most susceptible to theft of equipment but not to criminal damage; cabin cruisers and dinghies were slightly more popular targets for vandals. Overall though, there was evidence that thieves favour locations rather than particular types of boat. Most crime is committed in harbours (a major reason why Dorset figures are higher than those for Jersey is that more boats are moored in harbours in the former), but numerically more boats are moored here. Proportionally more crime is committed against boats at river/canal moorings, boatyards and, to a slightly lesser extent, coastal moorings. Basic security measures at all these locations were poor. They were better at marinas where less crime was reported although the safest place to keep a boat is at home (including garage/lock up).

Individual boat-related security measures appeared to be unsuccessful in preventing crime, although this finding should be treated with caution since it is possible that in some instances measures were taken following a crime. In some cases security measures may have escalated the level of damage as determined thieves sought to circumvent them. Similarly, there was no evidence that boat and equipment marking affected the levels of boat crime. However, there were some positive findings for other security measures.

There was a little evidence that membership of a marking scheme reduced the risk of crime[9] specifically with regard to outboard motors. Moreover, those who were members of boat watch schemes, particularly in Dorset harbours, reported fewer thefts in all categories. This is especially true regarding theft of equipment. However, these findings are presented tentatively. The numbers involved are too small for one to do more, but it is a base on which further studies may build.

Respondents who had joined the Merchant Shipping Register and the Small Ships Register were lukewarm when asked about their usefulness. Nevertheless, the majority of all respondents were in favour of a national shipping register, suggesting that the rejection of this by official bodies may be premature. There is certainly some merit in bringing the registers under one authority but, again, more research is needed on this.

Overall this study has shown that theft of and from, and damage to, boats is considerably higher than statistics suggest, and that certain boat owners are especially vulnerable. There is some evidence of the benefits of some types of security measures in certain circumstances. What is required is a more focused and detailed project aimed at building on the findings here. Maritime crime remains under-recorded and under-researched. Until these deficiencies are rectified the evidence suggests that there will continue to be victims, and that there will continue to be boat owners employing inappropriate responses, some of which may even make the problem worse.

Discussion

Q. Why have criminologists taken so little interest in maritime crime? After all, it is not just boat owners who suffer. Maritime frauds can send businesses into liquidation, and terrorism and piracy can result in deaths.

A. The study of crime has adopted a rather narrow focus. There are lots of studies of the Home Office police, but very few studies of other types of police officers or of people serving police functions, for example private police groups. Moreover, business crime and crimes that occur at the workplace have, until recently, received very little attention. So it is not just maritime crime that has been ignored. In reality it is much easier to get funds to research prisons, juvenile crime and drugs than it is to research maritime crime issues. I find the maritime crime

---

[9] Numbers were too small to comment on the extent to which marking improved the chances of goods being recovered.

community unsupportive of research initiatives. This is something Tim Goodhead will refer to in the next paper.

Q. I was interested in your comment that two-thirds of boat owners were in favour of national registration. This is a very important finding. Do you think this justifies compulsory registration?

A. Not in itself, but it does highlight the need for more research. In this relatively short questionnaire I did not enquire into the advantages and disadvantages or the strength of feeling on the matter. My findings suggest that such an enquiry would be instructive.

Q. That vessels moored in some locations are more vulnerable than others needs more thought. Have the police and security companies shown much interest in your findings?

A. Some have shown considerable interest. Only time will tell how successful the findings will be in influencing people. Certainly, I have found considerable scope for optimism.

Maritime crime—a boat owner's perspective

Tim Goodhead

Other papers have already made reference to the distinct lack of knowledge on the scale of maritime crime. The police records that do exist are collated at a regional level and not nationally. In addition, the records that are kept are administered in different ways. It is almost impossible to build up a national picture from official statistics. Nevertheless, local information is available and it is proving very instructive. For example, statistics released by the Hampshire Constabulary indicate that boats and equipment worth well in excess of £1 million were stolen from the county in 1992. Moreover, this is unquestionably an underestimate since much criminal activity—and vandalism is a case in point—is not included in these figures.

Indeed, vandalism is an unfortunate part of modern life. In a marine context this is especially common where people, and this includes water enthusiasts, meet to socialise by the water's edge. Excessive alcohol consumption all too frequently can lead to the damage of near-by marine craft and equipment for 'fun'. This may be accentuated by the 'edge syndrome': people enjoy leisure walking on beaches and river estuaries, etc. However, a very small percentage are, or become, vandals. It is worth mentioning here that since most people who enjoy the sea do so from the land, it is sometimes difficult to draw the parameters for maritime crime. Indeed, someone from a London Chinese restaurant was recently caught stealing carp. This is the wrong place to debate whether that is maritime crime or not, but it is an interesting point.

In a similar way it is often difficult to draw distinctions between vandalism and theft. For example, when is damage to a cabin door criminal damage and when is it a consequence of an attempted burglary? Much theft does occur and frequently it happens because the thief sees an opportunity. Unfortunately, where there are boats there is plenty of opportunity. Thieves see unsecured equipment and find the temptation too strong. In areas such as the River Hamble in Hampshire there is a high density of boats. Thus, a thief with self-confidence can find, with relative ease, a power boat on a trailer that is not secured, hitch it up to his car and drive it to another region of the country. It can then be sold on with little chance of detection. Indeed, there have been instances of thieves driving into boatyards, dismantling parts of boats and taking them away. Recently, somebody drove a van into Port Solent and spent hours dismantling the outdrives and the engine installation from a power boat. The specific nature of the parts taken fuels the impression that goods are being stolen to order.

A recent phenomenon in the United Kingdom has been the growth of boat jumbles. Many a cynic wonders where so much equipment at the larger shows comes from. There is a widely held belief that they are a repository for stolen goods, but there is no hard evidence at present that the majority of the equipment is being sold other than honestly. Many small items of marine equipment are sold through local papers and notice boards but again it is extremely difficult to check ownership.

The sale of stolen goods from yachts and boats is relatively easy, but it is harder when dealing with a large vessel where the purchaser will enquire into its history. Larger vessels that have been stolen have been traced abroad and once a boat reaches the Mediterranean and has been re-sprayed it may be lost for ever. Peter Clark has commented on this and so I will focus more on the domestic scene.

What is being done? Researching into this issue is problematic. Recently, a research assistant, Nicholas Kasic, and I attempted to conduct a survey of boat owners' attitudes to the security of their vessels. Our approaches met with silence. This is partly because security is perceived as a sensitive issue. In addition, security is seen as a low priority by those who own boats. In this paper I shall attempt to evaluate the view, which is widely held, that boat owners are unconcerned with the security of their vessels. I shall argue that this apparent disinterest, if it exists, may in fact reflect a conscious decision. I will also say something about developments in crime prevention as they apply to the local boating scene.

It is thought by many that registration might provide an answer to some of the problems of maritime crime. Indeed, there is a belief that registration might act as both a deterrent to thieves and an aid to identification of goods recovered after theft. Many harbour authorities and river authorities have a registration scheme as part of their harbour dues collection activities. In addition, many private schemes are in evidence. Usually details of boats are held on computer and stickers are issued to advertise this. The most effective form of registration in terms of crime prevention appears to be the boat watch schemes. These are a copy of the neighbourhood watch system. They involve a commitment to collective vigilance combined with a register. While police crime prevention officers are frequently involved in setting up the schemes, the onus is very much on the marine community to ensure their successful operation.

I personally do not believe that these schemes are necessary, and for several reasons. First, there is the point that they are superfluous. For example, sailing crafts such as Toppers or Lasers already have identification numbers. From these numbers insurance companies will have a good idea which vessels are stolen. Indeed, they provide a list of stolen boats and offer rewards for those that are regained. All that this system requires is the recording of the identification numbers. In any event a register already exists for small ships at the Driver Vehicle Licensing Centre at Swansea.

Second, in some cases there are practical difficulties. For example, the latest form of registration involves the tagging of equipment and boats. Electronic tags are buried in the boat or equipment and can be read with a microwave scanner. There are several systems on the market and this leads to practical problems in that the police would need to equip themselves with a large selection of scanners in order to deal with the problem comprehensively. The tagging concept is backed by a number of privately owned registers. These systems are likely to become increasingly sophisticated.

Third, registration would be too complex. It is not as straightforward as registering cars. The problem is akin to that of creating a dog register. There are many 'cross breeds' and thus identification is very difficult. Fourth, the Royal Yachting Association—a recognised champion of education rather than legislation—has pointed out that the seas are about freedom. A register is incompatible with this aim. Fifth, the problem with a formal register is that it invites taxation. This has occurred in other European countries and boat owners are genuinely concerned about this. Further worries are that a licensing system for boats might follow if a register was set up. Sixth, there is a concern about the cost, and this has a number of aspects.

The relatively low value of some equipment such as windsurfers might make the cost of registration prohibitive. The cost of registration also has to be compared with the cost of insurance and the cost of security. For example, it will cost £30 to insure a Laser sailing dinghy with a value of £1,000. This is so low that, unless the insurance company is insistent, it is a disincentive for the owner to worry about registration. Similarly, the cost of security for such a boat is high compared with the cost of insurance. A quality padlock and chain may cost as much as £40. Clearly this is more than the insurance premium. Thus, to return to the thesis I mentioned earlier, while at first sight it may appear that the boat owner is apathetic towards security it could reasonably be argued that the low cost of insurance policies has enabled owners to shift the risk; they appear to be making a sound financial decision.

Moreover, while Martin Gill's findings (in the previous paper) suggest that victimisation may be high, often the amounts lost are quite small. In other words some boat owners perceive there to be a low risk of costly crimes being committed against their vessels. Official statistics collected by Chichester Police offer some support for this idea. For the first six months of 1993 the police note that the value of marine equipment stolen from the Chichester Harbour area amounted to £36,177. They estimate the total value of yachts and equipment there are at £77 million. Of course bland statements such as this may disguise real differences. Indeed, Martin Gill's study shows that boats moored in particular locations, for example boat yards or river and canal moorings, are especially vulnerable. Nevertheless, losses are not perceived to be great. This is certainly an area which would benefit from further research.

However, one has to be careful when working out cost that one defines the boundaries. Often the problem of a theft is not so much the cost of the item stolen as the consequential costs. The loss of fishing tackle can be crucial to those who make their living from fishing. Similarly, within the leisure industry, the boating season is relatively short and theft/damage to a boat may result in the owner losing the best part of the season. This is a factor that is difficult to weigh.

A further point is that the chances of having stolen goods returned, or of bringing about a successful prosecution of vandals and thieves are slight. Policing large expanses of coast, river and estuaries is a difficult and an extremely expensive operation. I have even heard the view expressed that crimes against boat owners should be classified as a low priority either because boats are a luxury item or because boat owners can afford it. This is of course a gross injustice. It is surely a fundamental principle of our democracy that all are equal before the law. In any event some people are seriously hurt financially when a boat theft takes place. Their insurance policy will be invalid and they stand to lose tens of thousands of pounds. This is one strong argument for registration, but in my view it is outweighed by the disadvantages.

Registration of equipment might make more sense. With the growth of the boating industry there has been considerable development in the equipment area. Ten years ago some of the navigation equipment now to be found on a yacht would have been highly classified. Such things as Global Positioning Systems (GPS) are relatively commonplace nowadays. Modern electronic equipment is highly portable and it is installed in flimsy glass fibre boats.

This combination makes the technology very attractive to the thief. Moreover, the modern boat with its equipment is often housed in a marina which by its very nature has to allow relatively open access from the sea and the land. Marinas could provide more security but once Colditz-style guarding was installed the character of a marina would be destroyed. Some measures are unsightly and a balance needs to be struck.

Some boat owners mistakenly believe that once they are moored in a marina responsibility for their vessel is transferred to the marina authorities. However, as in car parks the liability rests with the owners. Indeed, this parallel is worth highlighting because many of the security measures which are now being seen as appropriate for marinas have been installed in car parks. A case in point is the closed circuit television camera. Cameras certainly have limitations in such large areas as marinas, but given the fact that they increase the amount of surveillance possible, they have a role to play. Controlling access is also crucial. Thieves and vandals can only steal if they have access. Technology has developed here too with the appearance of swipe cards on the main gates, or access is controlled by coded numbers. Often this is supplemented by padlocks and other physical security devices.

Throughout Europe there is a wide variety of alarms and monitoring devices available to the boat owner. Some are very sophisticated and involve radio links with central base stations. Systems can provide information on intruders, fire, flood, battery power, emergency and vessel departure and arrival. Thus, they offer safety as well as crime prevention capabilities.

Electronic systems can be complemented by technology similar to that used for home security. The basic problem is that boats move and are prone to extreme conditions. Devices such as infra red sensors and vibration pads are often not suitable for the marine environment. The problem is accentuated by the fact that, without back-up support, when alarms do sound the response time is very slow. If an alarm goes off in the middle of an estuary it is unlikely that much attention will be paid to it and the process of tracing an owner is often lengthy.

There is a large number of disabling devices on the market for everything from trailer hitches to engines. This is a relatively inexpensive way of protecting equipment although it probably does little more than displace the crime to another vessel. Going a stage further and providing secure padlocks and security fences is problematic. As I noted earlier, the modern boat is a fairly fragile structure, and there is little point putting expensive locks on the main hatchway when it is a relatively simple matter to make a hole in the structure with a sledge hammer. There is one school of thought that advocates providing the minimum in terms of security so that if the boat is broken into structural damage is kept to the minimum. In other words, one method of crime prevention is to refrain from using security devices at all.

In other words there are quite sound reasons why boat owners may not place great emphasis on security. As I have shown, there is certainly no lack of security equipment on the market, either for boats or marinas. The problem is that we have little knowledge about its effectiveness. Indeed, we still know very little about marine crime, about the type of people who become victims and the circumstances which encourage it. Some potential remedies—and registration is a case in point—have not been fully evaluated. Offering registration as a solution to marine crime is simplistic in the extreme when we know so little about the phenomenon. The risks of crime are not readily apparent, but the potential a register offers to the Inland Revenue most definitely is. What is needed is a more comprehensive understanding of the problem. The indications are that official statistics understate the scale of maritime crime.

A rough cost-benefit analysis by the boat owner may show that it is better to rely on insurance policies than incur the costs of providing additional security. There appear to be exceptions where sophisticated systems incorporate a safety feature as well. In this area there are many exciting developments. Some form of identification of equipment is essential if the police are to take action. This may be as simple as post coding or as sophisticated as tagging. In the long term, registration may hit the boating world through European Union harmonisation, but at the moment there are a number of organisations fulfilling this role. For the boat owner, there is a trade-off between increased security and possible central government intervention. At present, voluntary self-help schemes, in conjunction with the local police force coupled to a VHF system, seems to be the most successful solution to this growing problem.

Discussion

Q. In your paper you pointed out that you were against the registration of boats but saw merit in registration of equipment. Are you positively in favour of this idea, and why?

A. Marking equipment with a post code or electronic tag is a relatively cheap way of assisting the police to trace owners of equipment. Registration of boats would add to costs but realise very few benefits for the boat owner.

Q. I think you raise an interesting dilemma when you argue against registration on the basis of security. That I understand, but what about safety? Is it not the case that registration would make our seas much safer?

A. The registration of pleasure craft for commercial purposes is presently being discussed. This may be the start of another movement to register all boats. However, in terms of safety it is the crew not the boat that perhaps needs to be prioritised.

Q. Following on from the last question, you said that a licensing system for boating competence might follow a register. Is that not a very good idea if the aim is to make the water and seas a safer place?

A. Voluntary regulation through education rather than legislation seems eminently sensible to me.

Q. In your paper you mentioned that we ought to make owners more aware of the problems, or at least that was a theme that I think emerged. Is anything being done about this? If so, what?

A. Marine watch schemes initiated by crime prevention officers are providing the best means of making the boat owner more aware of criminal activity.

Index

Arson, 14

Container crime, 21–28
   cost, 21
   limitations of seals, 23–24
Criminal damage, 48, 50, 55
Customs & Excise, 29–38

Drug trafficking, 3, 13, 29, 30–36

Far East Regional Investigating Team (FERIT), 8
Fraud, 2, 4, 14–15, 24, 25

Insurance companies, 12, 20, 27, 42–43, 60
International Association of Air Port and Sea Port Police, 9
International Chamber of Commerce, 9
International Maritime Bureau, 1, 9, 25
International Maritime Organisation, 1, 9

Marine Accidents Investigation Board, 14
Maritime crime
   and containers, 21–28
   and Customs & Excise, 29–38
   costs of, 4
   defined, 1, 58
   international dimensions of, 4–11
   investigating, loss adjustment, 12–20
   prevention, 39–46
   victimisation
     of boat owners, 47–57, 58–64
Murder, 7

National Association of Marine Investigators, 17

Phantom ships, 8
Piracy, 2, 9–10
Police, 1, 17, 31, 37
   Dutch, 9

Essex Police Marine Unit, 39
Interpol, 9, 17
Mariner Computer Database, 13
perspectives on crime prevention, 44
Proksch, Udo, 6

Registers
   British Ships Register, 14
   International Yacht Registry, 10
   Merchant Shipping Register, 53, 56
   Small Ships Register, 14, 20, 41, 53, 56, 60
Registration, 13, 16, 18, 41, 43, 53, 59, 60, 61, 63
Royal Yachting Association (RYA), 41

Scuttling, 7–8, 14–15
Security measures, 13, 48, 51, 52, 55
   boat marking, 52–53
   CCTV, 51, 62
   Global Positioning Systems (GPS), 61
   hull identification number, 16
   Marine watch, 42, 59
   tagging, 44, 60, 63

Theft, 12–14, 50
   recovery rates, 13

Perpetuity Press specialises in publications relating to crime, security, criminal justice, law and related topics. It publishes academic texts, as well as popular reading, and professional and in-house magazines. Individuals or companies requiring further information should contact

*Perpetuity Press
PO Box 376
Leicester
LE2 3ZZ
Telephone: (0116) 2704186*

Also published by Perpetuity Press:

Crime at Work: studies in security and crime prevention

Edited by Martin Gill

Topics covered include: robbery; commercial burglary; ram raiding; shoplifting; insurance fraud; violence against staff; crime on industrial estates; fiddling in hotel bars; terrorism and the retail sector; the effectiveness of Electronic Article Surveillance; customer and staff perceptions of Closed Circuit Television; security implementation in a security environment; and the advantages of in-house to contract security staff.

(230 pages, index included)

Crime and Security: managing the risk to safe shopping

by Adrian Beck and Andrew Willis

Topics covered include: the extent and nature of crime and nuisance in town centres and shopping centres; ways of responding to crime and nuisance and the priority given to creating a risk-free environment; the role and control of private security guards; the use and effectiveness of closed circuit television; security shutters and designing-out crime; and the development of an integrated security strategy for safe shopping.

(To be published April 1995
approximately 160 pages, index included)

Crime and Security Shorter Studies Series
Public Order Policing:
contemporary perspectives on strategy and tactics
by Mike King and Nigel Brearley

Topics covered include: the nature of crowds; police policy and training practices; developments in strategy and tactics; the policing of political; industrial; festival and urban public order events; and incorporates results of interviews with senior operational police trainers and practitioners.

(To be published June 1995
approximately 100 pages, index and glossary of terms included)

Perpetuity Press